Catherine t

Michael Streeter

HAUS PUBLISHING · LONDON

First published in Great Britain in 2007 by
Haus Publishing Limited
26 Cadogan Court
Draycott Avenue
London SW3 3BX

www.hauspublishing.co.uk

Copyright © Michael Streeter, 2007

The moral rights of the author have been asserted

A CIP catalogue record for this book is available from the British Library

ISBN 978-1-905791-06-4

Typeset in Garamond 3 by MacGuru Ltd
info@macguru.org.uk

Printed in Dubai by Oriental Press

Front cover: *Catherine the Great* by Vigilius Erichsen courtesy akg Images
Back cover: *Catherine the Great* by Fedor Rokotov courtesy Getty Images

Catherine the Great

Contents

The German Princess 1729–45

When Sophia Augusta Fredericka arrived into the world on 21 April 1729, few could have predicted a great future for the fair-skinned, blue-eyed baby.[1] It was true that Sophia, whose birthplace was the Baltic Sea port of Stettin in Pomerania – now Szczecin in Poland – was fortunate enough to be born into a noble family. Her father was Prince Christian August of Anhalt-Zerbst while her mother was Princess Johanna Elizabeth of Holstein-Gottorp. Sophia herself was therefore a princess. That, however, was almost the limit of her good fortune.

For one thing, Sophia's family had very little money. The reason she was born in Stettin was that her father was a serving officer in the Prussian army, and it was in that town on the River Oder that he had been placed in charge of the garrison. Moreover the prince owned few lands in his own Anhalt-Zerbst, a tiny principality about 70 miles southwest of Berlin, and though he later became its ruler he had virtually no real political influence. It was just one of many such tiny states and principalities that made up what is now Germany and Sophia was just one among many princesses born into small German principalities at this time. She could expect to inherit very little in her own right; and certainly not the throne of a great nation.

However, Sophia's family did have one great advantage, especially on her mother's side – and that was connections. These connections, coupled with her own considerable abilities and

It was in 1739, when Catherine was just ten, that she first met the man who was to be her husband. Duke Karl Peter of Holstein-Gottorp was her second cousin and was just a year older than Sophia. Peter certainly had an impressive pedigree. His father, who had recently died, was Karl Frederick, Duke of Holstein-Gottorp, nephew of Charles XII of Sweden. Karl Peter, therefore, had every prospect of one day becoming the king of Sweden. However, the 11-year-old also had a more direct and even more illustrious forbear. Peter the Great's daughter by his second wife Catherine was Anna Petrovna, who had later married Karl Frederick. The young Duke Karl Peter was their son. This made Karl Peter a grandson of Peter the Great. However, thanks to the late Emperor's tinkering with the issue of succession in Russia, the young Duke was by no means assured of attaining the imperial throne even if he had a strong claim to it.

Already there was gossip at court that Sophia and Karl, both still children, could one day make a good match. For Sophia – and especially her mother Johanna Elizabeth – the prospect of this impoverished princess becoming the Queen of Sweden one day must have been an enticing one. Sophia's own reaction to this first meeting with Karl Peter at Eutin in 1739 was mixed. In the first draft of her much-amended memoirs Sophia was to write that the young duke *truly was handsome, amiable, and well-mannered; indeed, they hailed this eleven-year-old child, whose father*

Peter the Great (1672–1725), or Peter I as he was officially known, is generally credited with helping to make Russia a world power, most notably in Europe, where his victory over Sweden gave Russia access to the Baltic Sea. A powerfully-built man, he could be ruthless with anyone who stood in the way of his desire to modernise and Westernise the country. He even had his own son Alexei tortured for disobedience, a punishment that killed him. Among his more positive achievements were the founding of the Russian navy, the reorganisation of the shambolic Russian state and the founding of a new capital – St Petersburg. He changed the law to allow emperors to nominate their own successors.

Peter the Great, the founder of modern Russia. Triumphantly depicted here revealing his plans for the city of St Petersburg

had just died, as a miracle. However, this passage was subsequently omitted and Sophia's remaining comments were rather less flattering. *In truth, his face was pale in colour and he seemed to be thin and of a delicate constitution*, she wrote. She also referred to his reputation for liking alcohol. *From the age of ten {he} was partial to drink.*[4]

Sophia was still very young at the time she first met Karl Peter. However, she was to grow up quite quickly, emotionally and physically, in the next few years. In 1742 her father had a stroke that briefly left him paralysed down one side. Worse was to follow when her brother William, who had never been strong, died at the age of 12. Johanna Elizabeth was utterly distraught at the loss. Meanwhile Prince Christian August had with his brother inherited the position of joint ruler of Anhalt-Zerbst, which meant that he resigned his military position and the family moved from Stettin back to his native Zerbst. It was at this time that the 13-year-old Sophia met a remarkable woman who was quite unlike anyone she had previously encountered. She was the 30-year-old Countess of Bentinck, a liberated woman, separated from her husband and who apparently had a son by one of her footman. She may even have had a female lover. The Countess was a spontaneous person and an excellent horsewoman who rose astride like a man. It seems that the older woman's overt sensuality, boldness and freedom of spirit made a lasting impression on the young Sophia; at the very least it may have kindled her great passion for riding. Indeed, her love of riding and her self-confessed liking for riding astride pillows in her bed are often seen as evidence of Sophia's growing awareness of her own sensuality at this time.[5]

Sophia was by now growing into an increasingly attractive young woman, no great beauty certainly, but she was tall, had a good figure, an intelligent face and a pleasing smile. Meanwhile, many miles away in Russia, events were taking place that were to have a fundamental impact on the young German princess's life. In late 1741 Peter the Great's daughter Elizabeth had seized power, deposing the infant Emperor Ivan VI and proclaiming herself Empress.

Having no legitimate heir of her own, Elizabeth searched around for someone she could name as her successor. Her choice was Sophia's cousin, Karl Peter, Duke of Holstein and already heir to the Swedish crown as well as being a grandson of Peter the Great and Elizabeth's nephew. In November 1742 the young Duke was proclaimed heir to the Russian throne. As part of this process the Duke became the Grand Duke, changed his name to Peter Fyodorovich and had to change religions from the Lutheran to the Russian Orthodox Church. The Duke was also made to renounce his claim to the Swedish throne. As a result of this Adolf Frederick of Holstein-Gottorp, the Prince-Bishop of Lübeck, was named as successor to that title.

Both developments were of huge importance to Sophia and her family. Adolf Frederick was Johanna Elizabeth's brother, while Sophia's name had already been linked with the youth who was now heir to the mighty Russian throne. Moreover, Johanna Elizabeth had

Empress Elizabeth Petrovna (1709–61) was another of Peter the Great's daughters by his second wife (who ruled 1725–7 as Catherine I and who was the daughter of a peasant). Elizabeth seized power from the infant Emperor Ivan VI in 1741 and was generally regarded as a relatively benign ruler who abolished capital punishment. Although extravagant in some of her tastes, and naturally lazy, she was also seen as a strong Russian patriot – and pious devotee of the Orthodox Church – who had helped reduce German influence at court. She is thought to have secretly married her Ukrainian Cossack lover Alexei Razumovsky but officially was unmarried and had no heir of her own.

an existing connection with the new Empress of Russia. Some years before, Elizabeth had been engaged to be married to another of Johanna Elizabeth's brothers, Karl August, though he had died of smallpox. Johanna Elizabeth had already made full use of her connections, and had written to the Empress to congratulate her on her accession to the Russian throne. She was quick to remind her of their existing ties and by 1743 had sent a portrait of her daughter Sophia to the court at St Petersburg. The portrait seems to have gone down well. In these, the highest of marriage stakes, little could be left to chance and Johanna was proving skilful at promoting her daughter.

Even so, just as Sophia's prospects of marrying into the Russian imperial family seemed to be growing, her fortunes came close to taking another and altogether less promising turn. Yet another of her mother's brothers, Georg-Ludwig, who was only ten years older than Sophia, had fallen in love with her. The still-innocent Sophia herself seems only to have belatedly realised the nature of his affections, though it is unclear just how much Johanna Elizabeth initially realised what was going on – or even whether she encouraged it. The outcome seems to have been that in 1743 Sophia – who found her uncle good-looking though she did not love him – agreed to marry Georg-Ludwig, on the condition that her parents (Georg's sister and brother-in-law) agreed.

Here this strange affair languished until the beginning of January 1744 when Johanna Elizabeth received a letter from the Russian court. It was an invitation for Johanna Elizabeth and her daughter Sophia to visit Russia, ostensibly to give them a chance to pay their respects to the Empress, and for the Empress to thank the mother for her past kindness. In reality of course the true purpose of the request was very clear – Sophia was being lined up to become Grand Duke Peter's bride, subject to his and the Empress' final approval once they had met her. Yet though this seemed to be the successful culmination of Johanna Elizabeth's scheming on

A portrait of the Empress Catherine in the early years of her reign

behalf of her 14-year-old daughter, it was at this moment that the mother wavered. Her first reaction when she discussed the issue with Sophia was concern over the likely reaction of her younger brother Georg-Ludwig. This was a curious response from a woman who had actively encouraged Sophia's marriage chances at the Russian court. Johanna Elizabeth also now claimed that Russia was an unstable and dangerous place for someone as young and unworldly as Sophia to venture. Yet that country was no more dangerous now than it had been in 1743 when Johanna Elizabeth had dispatched the portrait of Sophia there.

It could be that Johanna Elizabeth had been genuinely concerned for her brother Georg-Ludwig's feelings, even though any marriage of his to Sophia would have needed church approval because of their close blood ties – even assuming that Christian August would have given his permission. Another theory is that Johanna Elizabeth had started to see her increasingly mature daughter as a rival and resented the fact that though the Russian court had invited both of them, it was really only Sophia in whom they would be interested. This indeed would prove to be the case. However Sophia herself brushed aside Georg-Ludwig's feelings, informing her mother that if he really cared about her, her uncle could *wish only for her fortune and well-being.* This was an early glimpse of the steely resolve that Sophia would show in later life when faced with difficult and often dangerous situations.[6] It also suggested that now that the prospect of such an exalted marriage was a real one, the ambitious Sophia was determined not to let such a golden opportunity slip from her grasp, whatever the concerns of her mother.

Christian August was himself far from happy about his daughter's proposed journey to Russia, and as a devout Lutheran he was especially concerned about his daughter having to convert to the Orthodox faith if she became betrothed to the heir to the Russian throne. Yet nevertheless he gave permission for his wife and Sophia to make the journey in January 1744. Both he and Sophia must have realised that this would probably be the last time they would ever see each other.

Christian August accompanied his wife and daughter as far as Berlin, where he said his last farewell to Sophia and gave her a set of written instructions as to her future conduct. Meanwhile instructions of a different kind were given to Johanna Elizabeth by the Prussian king Frederick II – the Great – who, despite the supposed secrecy of the journey, knew its real purpose perfectly well. He asked Johanna Elizabeth effectively to work as his unofficial agent in Russia, to help further the Prussian cause wherever possible. The King also took the opportunity to meet Sophia, whose marriage he hoped would help Prussia, and was impressed with her. Curiously, Johanna Elizabeth tried unsuccessfully to prevent this meeting. Indeed from now on the actions of her mother would be as much a hindrance as a help to Sophia.

Travelling eastwards to and then across Russia in the middle of winter was no easy matter. It was a long, bitterly cold and arduous journey, even at a time when people were used to measuring journeys by days rather than by hours and when even the best roads were difficult in poor weather. Yet it was also a valuable early lesson for Sophia. Not only did it give her a first taste of the delights of Russian winters, it also gave her some idea of just how vast was the empire over which she would one day rule. For someone used to the relatively small size of German states and principalities, the sheer scale of the Russian lands must have been awe-inspiring.

Their aim was to make for Riga – where the Russian state began – and then on to the new capital St Petersburg founded by Peter the Great. Finally they were to head for the old capital Moscow where Elizabeth and the imperial court were staying. The hope was that they could reach Moscow by 9 February in time for the Grand Duke's birthday the following day. Eventually, after a frantic dash across the snow in huge sledges, mother and daughter finally made it in the early evening of 9 February and arrived at the Golovin Palace where they were met first by Grand Duke Peter and then by Empress Elizabeth. This was the first chance for the Empress to vet the future bride of her heir, and an opportunity for Peter to become reacquainted with Sophia after nearly five years. She seemed to make a favourable impression on them both, and the Empress even seemed pleased with Johanna Elizabeth – though

A print of a Moscow street scene in the years of Catherine the Great's rule. She disliked staying in the ramshackle and chaotic city

their relationship would soon become strained. At the same time it was a chance for the young German princess to see the Empress, her intended husband, and the court and way of life that would soon be hers. Sophia seems to have been very impressed by the magnificently-attired and diamond-bedecked Empress, whom she described as *a large woman who, in spite of being very stout, was not in the least disfigured by her size nor was she embarrassed in her movements. Her head, too, was very beautiful.* In fact the only thing that detracted from her looks, felt Sophia, was her 'potato' nose.[7]

The pragmatic Sophia threw herself into her new life in the goldfish bowl of Russian court life, where she was quickly aware that every move made by her and the Grand Duke was being watched. She was determined to become fluent in Russian and seems to have been a willing and able pupil, even if she never lost her German accent. The Princess was also assiduous in learning about the Orthodox Church to which she would convert in preparation for marrying into the imperial family. Indeed, her biggest problem was not her new environment, but her mother. Johanna Elizabeth found it hard to come to terms with playing a minor role compared with that of her daughter. Perhaps to compensate for her relative unimportance, Johanna Elizabeth became involved in court politics, intriguing with those in the court who favoured stronger links with Prussia and France. As all correspondence was routinely intercepted and read, this meddling did not the escape the notice of Count Alexei Bestuzhev-Ryumin. He was the Empress' Vice-Chancellor and a powerful figure at court who was opposed to Prussian influence. As a result he was not keen on the Empress' choice of bride for the Grand Duke.

Sophia's mother was also judged to have shown a lack of maternal concern when the usually healthy princess was struck down by a serious illness in March 1744. This ailment was to leave the girl pale and painfully thin by the time her 15th birthday arrived. Nonetheless, Sophia had enhanced her reputation during her illness when she pointedly refused her mother's suggestion that a Lutheran pastor be fetched to comfort her, instead insisting on seeing an Orthodox priest, Simon Todorskii, the man instructing her in the new religion. It was an act calculated to delight the deeply pious Empress, as Sophia almost certainly knew it would. This was a clear sign that Sophia was already developing a skill that would help her enormously through the dangerous years ahead; an ability to know what she needed to say and do to keep powerful people happy.

The Empress' admiration for the seriousness with which Sophia was adapting to her new life easily outweighed her growing disdain for her mother and her intrigues, and by May 1744 Christian August was formally asked permission for his daughter to become betrothed. Though the Prince had serious qualms, especially about his daughter's imminent conversion to the Orthodox Church, there was never much chance that he would defy the

Russian throne and say no. Meanwhile Sophia, though herself a sincere Lutheran, seems to have been able to justify her conversion on the grounds that behind their very different exterior trappings, the two belief systems were not fundamentally so very far apart. She was also probably astute enough to perceive that Peter, whom she said *clung to Lutheranism* even though he had himself converted, had not made many friends by his antipathy towards the faith of his future subjects.[8]

Sophia was formally converted to Orthodoxy on 28 June in the chapel of the Golovin Palace in Moscow, and the next day she and Peter were officially betrothed. Both ceremonies were fabulously elaborate and exhausting. Following her betrothal the German princess was now a Grand Duchess, while thanks to her conversion she was to be known by her new name Catherine (Ekaterina in Russian), chosen by the Empress in honour of her own mother Catherine I. The new Grand Duchess was given a small household of her own and an annual allowance of 30,000 roubles, though Catherine, who enjoyed spending money, always found it hard to live within her means. Nonetheless, in theory all seemed set fair for Catherine and the future of the Russian imperial house. After all, the Empress had her heir and had now found an attractive and healthy fiancée for him, someone from an obscure German family with no complications in her background.

Yet despite this promising start to her new life, there were difficult, even dangerous times ahead for Catherine. Her presence in Russia depended utterly on Peter, and late in 1744 the often sickly young man contracted a series of illnesses that culminated in smallpox. When Catherine saw Peter after his recovery she realised her future husband had been badly marked by the disease. *He had become hideous*, Catherine later wrote.[9] Yet though his physical shortcomings may have made Peter harder for Catherine to love, they paled alongside the problems caused by their very different personalities. For despite a promising start, and the fact that her very existence in Russia depended on Peter, theirs would be a relationship that the young Catherine would find increasingly difficult to bear.

An Unsuitable Match 1745–60

In theory Catherine and Peter had much in common and in many ways they should have been the suitable match that Empress Elizabeth had intended. They were of a similar background, spoke the same languages, had shared the same faith and were close in age. Moreover they had both been thrust into the intensity of the Russian court with its spies, surveillance, opulent ways and strange customs, and had both been compelled to adopt a new faith and learn a new language in a new country. And initially at least the similarity of their positions did throw the young pair together as they became friends in adversity.

However, they were such very different personalities with such very different approaches to life, that it is hardly surprising that their relationship barely got beyond the level of childhood companions. Eventually they would come to live almost entirely separate lives. Catherine, though still innocent in many ways, was quick to learn from the world around her, was intelligent if not an intellectual, understood what motivated people, and set out to make as good an impression of herself as possible to the Russian court in general and the Empress in particular. Her progress in learning the Russian language was just one sign of this dedication to her role. Peter, in contrast, was a young man who did not understand how to win allies and influence people. He never grasped how his often boorish words and acts affected other people; for example he made little effort to hide his disdain for Russia in contrast with

Catherine II's husband, the unfortunate and doomed Peter III

his zeal for all things Prussian. Though he was far from stupid, and had an appreciation of music, the Grand Duke was slow to mature physically and above all emotionally. One of his great passions – apart from drinking – was for all things military. He did not just play with toy soldiers but made his servants dress up in military uniforms and parade, and gave them titles or promoted them according to his mood.

Catherine seems to have tried to make their relationship work – even if true love was never a possibility– while for his part Peter had respect for the Grand Duchess and her obvious intelligence. But the imperial heir's immaturity made it hard for her. In her admittedly tendentious memoirs written later Catherine said of Peter at this time: *In general he was very much still a child, although he turned sixteen in 1744 when the Russian court was in Moscow.* She was also taken aback, she claims, when he revealed that he was in love with one of the Empress' maids of honour, and that while he was grateful he could 'open his heart' to his second cousin, he was only marrying Catherine because his aunt – the Empress – wanted him to. *Deep in my heart I was astonished by his imprudence and lack of judgement in many matters,* she wrote.[10]

In the months before the wedding Catherine appears to have suffered some anxiety, even if there is no sign that she was having a serious change of heart about marrying a man she did not find physically or emotionally attractive. In any case there was little time to dwell on doubts as, with the Grand Duke's health still poor, the Empress was keen that they should get married as soon as possible – and produce a heir. The wedding was eventually set for 21 August 1745 and was held in the Church of Our Lady of Kazan in St Petersburg. It was another magnificent occasion, which started early with the firing of cannons at 5 a.m. The procession to the church featured dragoons, horse guards, hussars, court officials and numerous coaches and it took the Empress and the betrothed couple three hours to travel the short distance to the church in

Elizabeth's own barn-like carriage. After the long ceremony there was a celebration at the Winter Palace which included a lavish dinner followed by a ball. The newlyweds were later ceremonially led to their bedchamber by the Empress where they were formally attired in their nightclothes – and then left alone.

There is little doubt that Catherine and Peter's marriage was not consummated on that night or indeed any night for a long time. It is even just possible – though unlikely – that it was never consummated at all. On that first evening Peter left his new bride alone in their bed while he enjoyed a late supper, and then returned giggling, childishly amused at the thought of them being in bed together. He showed no interest in having a physical relationship with his wife either that night or for the remainder of the ten days of official wedding celebrations. According to her later writings, Catherine discovered that *my dear spouse paid absolutely no attention to me, but was constantly playing soldier with his valet.* Whether this was through natural shyness on Peter's part is unclear. There is some evidence that the young man may not have been physically developed enough at this point to enjoy normal sexual relations. What appeared to keep Catherine going both before and after the wedding was not physical but political desire. *As {the wedding} approached I grew more deeply melancholic. My heart did not foresee great happiness; ambition alone sustained me.*[11]

Although Catherine wrote these words years later and for posterity, they do suggest that she already foresaw a great future for herself. She also understood such a future could only be attained through her marriage to Peter. Indeed, even before her marriage the Grand Duchess had summarised the three strands of her strategy to win favour in Russia. This was to *please the Grand Duke*, to *please the Empress* and to *please the nation.*[12]

If Catherine was already starting to feel alone in her marriage with Peter then that loneliness increased in the autumn of 1745. First of all her mother Johanna Elizabeth left Russia, as there was no official reason for her to remain now that her daughter was married. In truth, Johanna Elizabeth had done Catherine as much harm as good in the last 18 months. Her self-centred behaviour, extravagant spending and an affair had not endeared her to the Russian court, while her attempts at political intrigues had stirred up anti-Prussian sentiments that did not make Catherine's life any easier. Yet Catherine was still only 16 and the departure of her mother – whom she would never see again – still came as a blow, despite their difficult relationship. *Her departure sincerely pained me; I cried a great deal*, Catherine wrote later. Soon afterwards she learnt to her horror that a favourite maid, Maria Zhukova, had been removed from her service. This hurtful act had – according to the Empress – been requested as a parting shot by Johanna Elizabeth on the grounds that the maid had got too close to her daughter. It may also have been the case that Empress Elizabeth simply wanted to show that she was in charge of Catherine. Either way the Grand Duchess was *profoundly pained* by this turn of events.[13]

The precariousness of Catherine's position and the extent to which she was at the mercy of the Empress and the imperial court was powerfully underlined during 1746. First of all, Peter was hit by another serious illness in the early spring, and though he recovered, Catherine had shown real concern for his survival. This concern stemmed not just from wifely devotion but also from the sure knowledge that if Peter died her position at the Russian court would be redundant. Then, once he had recovered from his illness, the childish Peter found that by drilling a hole into the wall of the Empress' private apartments he could spy on her and her friends as they relaxed in the evening. Elizabeth was furious when she discovered this juvenile prank, and raged at Peter – even suggesting he could meet the same grim fate as Peter the Great's son Alexei. Though Catherine was not implicated in this affair, it brought about a wholesale change in the so-called 'Young Court' of the newlyweds. Count Bestuzhev was ordered to draw up instructions for the supervision of the young imperial couple. Meanwhile a new woman was put in charge of Catherine, Maria Choglokova, a cousin of the Empress. The Grand Duchess took an immediate dislike to the new arrival, whom she later described as being *simpleminded, cruel, capricious, and very self-serving.* Her tears at this turn of events brought a reproach from Elizabeth herself; though Catherine mollified her by using a phrase she had recently found useful in placating the proud ruler: *I beg your pardon, mother.*[14]

Bestuzhev's instructions in relation to the Grand Duchess made it abundantly clear what her main role was – to produce a male heir as a matter of urgency. This was also said to be her main responsibility, rather than her husband's. It was also clear that one of Maria Choglokova's main tasks was to discover why there was no pregnancy so far. The simple reason for this was that Catherine and Peter were not having sex. Though this was clearly in large part down to Peter's lack of interest – and possibly a physical inability to have sexual intercourse at this time – Catherine appears equally to have shown little real inclination to force the issue. Even though Catherine was ambitious and felt she had a great future at the Russian court, she was still unwilling or unable to do the one thing that would ensure she would play a role in the imperial future – get pregnant. This was despite the likelihood that if she produced no children, her position and even her life could well be in danger. It would be a few years before the Grand Duchess would be able to find a solution to this matter.

Despite Catherine's precarious position, these were not entirely wasted years. Gradually in the late 1740s and early 1750s she began to develop one of her great passions – her love of reading. Initially she read only novels until they began to *bore* her; she then read the letters of Madame de Sévigné – which described the court of Louis XIV – and these she *devoured.* Later she moved on to the works of the philosopher and writer Voltaire, who would one day become a regular correspondent.[15] Catherine developed her love of riding too, and enjoyed hunting and shooting – pursuits in which she showed considerable ability. Catherine also liked dancing and particularly relished some of the masked balls put on by the Empress, including those where the women had to dress as men and the men as women. Both Elizabeth and Catherine – who was developing into an attractive young woman with a fine figure – looked good in men's clothes. At the same time Catherine was learning a great deal about the scale of the Russian empire and the variety of its lands and inhabitants as Elizabeth's court made regular processions around this vast country.

The Russian Empire at the end of the 1750s was already huge, stretching from Poland in the west to the Pacific Ocean to the east, and including the vast empty expanses of Siberia. Thanks to Peter the Great Russia had won access to the Baltic Sea via the Gulf of Finland; in the south its lands were close to the Black Sea which at that time was controlled by the Ottoman Empire. The thinly-spread population was little more than 15 million and were mostly made up of Slavs but also included Finns, Tartars, Bashkirs and other nationalities. The main religion was the Russian Orthodox Church but there were also Muslims in the south and many Lutherans in what are now Estonia and Latvia.

Catherine's life at this time was thus not perhaps quite as awful as her later memoirs might suggest. However, it was clear that for periods she was bored and frustrated. Then in March 1747 Catherine heard that her father had died. Catherine admitted that his death *deeply grieved me* and that *for a week I was allowed to cry as much as I wanted*. However, Maria Choglokova then informed her that the Empress demanded she stop crying on the grounds that, as the Grand Duchess put it, *my father had not been a king*.[16]

During this uncertain period Catherine missed the emotional companionship of a man. Her relationship with Peter had scarcely improved. He, too, had his own interests – hunting dogs, military paraphernalia and games, the violin, and drinking. Moreover he either did not know or did not care what impact his actions while drunk had on his young wife. One evening in 1750 a drunk Grand Duke flirted openly with the Duchess of Kurland, whom Catherine described as *neither beautiful nor pretty nor shapely – she was hunchbacked and rather small – but she had pretty eyes {and} intelligence*. Catherine retired early to bed and when Peter followed hours later he tried to get her attention to tell how much he liked his new friend. A proud Catherine seems to have been as much hurt by the pity shown by her maid over Peter's public flirting as she was by the flirting itself. She described her situation as being *as disagreeable as it was tedious*.[17]

Given that her marriage was an emotional void, it was not surprising that Catherine became involved in some, at first fairly harmless, flirtations of her own. These included a brief intrigue with Andrei Chernyshev, a member of the Grand Duke's entourage, who was later briefly interrogated over the matter and sent away from court. In 1751, his cousin, Count Zakhar Chernyshev, declared his passion for Catherine and the two exchanged letters. Indeed, Zakhar Chernyshev was one of a number of young Guards officers who Catherine had been discreetly cultivating; several of whom seem to have fallen in love with her. She was therefore adept at picking up important items of information about what was really going on at court. For example, when Elizabeth fell ill in early 1749, Catherine not only heard about it – even though the illness was kept quiet – she informed her husband and reassured him that should the Empress die, she knew several Guards officers who would support the pair's claim to the throne.

By the early 1750s, with the Empress' health uncertain and with still no sign of an heir from Peter and Catherine, pressure began to mount on the young couple. The Empress was furious when Maria Choglokova candidly admitted to her that the reason the young couple had not produced a child was because 'nothing had been done about it'.[18] Choglokova now decided to take more drastic measures. She arranged for a pretty young widow by the name

Sergei Saltykov was one of the earliest in a series of lovers that continued throughout Catherine the Great's life

of Madame Grooth to initiate Peter into the mysteries of sexual relations. Meanwhile since the spring of 1752 a handsome, rakish courtier called Sergei Saltykov had been displaying a keen interest in Catherine, and the still largely innocent 23-year-old gradually fell for him. Maria Choglokova may even have encouraged the courtier to continue their affair, though Peter and Catherine may also have consummated their marriage at last. In any case, whether or not Catherine and Peter were now having sex – no one can be sure if they did – Catherine at last got pregnant. She had her first miscarriage in December 1752 and another the following summer of 1753. By early 1754, however, she was pregnant again and this time she successfully gave birth. Her son Paul was born on 20 September 1754, a matter of huge relief for Catherine, Peter and of course a delighted Empress. At last the Grand Duchess had performed her duty and produced a male heir. No one can be sure whose son he was – Catherine certainly strongly hinted later he was not her husband's – though to a relieved Empress this probably mattered little. In the eyes of the world Paul would become the next in line to the imperial throne.

Despite her success in producing a male heir, Catherine soon felt more isolated than ever. For one thing she was allowed very little access to the infant. Paul had been whisked away from her immediately after the birth, while she was left alone in discomfort for several hours. She did not see him again for more than a month. Now that she had done her marital duty, Catherine was expected to fade discreetly into the background. Moreover the crucial mother–son bond was never allowed to develop as it might have done; and Catherine's long-term relationship with Paul probably suffered as a result. In hindsight, however, this period was a crucial turning point for Catherine. With the succession seemingly assured for the next generation, she could indeed have slipped quietly into obscurity at the Russian court, allowing her husband Peter and ultimately her son Paul to remain centre stage. Yet Catherine already had ambitions of her own, and these were to be more than simply the wife or mother of an emperor. She began to develop the skills and experience she would need to be a ruler.

Catherine had begun to learn the rudiments of statecraft through her husband, who had inherited administrative responsibilities as the Duke of Holstein. Though Catherine was not supposed to meddle in such political affairs, Peter sought her advice on matters relating to his authority there, respecting her good sense and attention to detail. She also seems to have been amused and secretly pleased when one of the imperial gardeners – who had predicted Elizabeth's own ascension to the throne – told the Grand Duchess that *I would become Sovereign Empress of Russia.*[19]

In that same year, 1755, a man arrived at the court who would become in effect Catherine's diplomatic tutor and help her develop her natural political skills. That man was the new British envoy Sir Charles Hanbury-Williams. Within the diplomat's entourage was another man who would also play an important role in Catherine's life; the young, romantic and idealistic Polish noble Count Stanislas August Poniatowski. The Pole quickly fell for Catherine's dazzling white complexion, dark hair and 'large expressive blooming blue eyes'. In turn, she fell for the charming aristocrat, and he became the first real love of her life.[20]

It was therefore during the second half of the 1750s that Catherine underwent her apprenticeship for the burdens of state that – she hoped – lay ahead. She received invaluable friendship and guidance (as well as money to pay her continuing debts) from the worldly-wise Hanbury-Williams, who clearly saw her potential, both personally and as a future ally of Great Britain. At the same time she was also moving closer to Count Bestuzhev, whom she now saw as the kind of important and powerful domestic figure she would need on her side. For his part the wily Count, though he had originally opposed Catherine's marriage to Peter, had come to regard her as someone who was both competent and who would put Russian interests first – unlike Peter, who rarely disguised his pro-Prussian sympathies. Catherine's growing sense that she was destined for greatness was clear. In a letter to Hanbury-Williams she described her feelings. *I would like to feel fear but I cannot; the invisible hand which has led me for thirteen years along a very rough road will never allow me to give way, of that I am very firmly and perhaps foolishly convinced.* In another letter she forecast that she would either *perish or reign.*[21]

These were certainly tense and dangerous times in the Russian court. One reason was increasing concern over the health of Elizabeth, prompting worries about the succession and the likely roles of Peter, Catherine and even the infant Paul. Officials such as Count Bestuzhev wanted to ensure that Catherine would be given a formal role in administration if and when Peter – who by this time also had his own lover– became emperor. Others – the rival Shuvalov faction, for example – were thought to want to skip a generation and establish a regency for the child Paul. That would be bad news for both Peter and Catherine. The other reason for the tension was the outbreak of the Seven Years War in Europe in 1756 which saw Russia allied with Austria, France and Sweden against Prussia and Great Britain.

This war split the Russian court, with Catherine and Bestuzhev opposed to the court's French-inclined factions led by the vice chancellor Michael Vorontsov and the current imperial favourite Ivan Shuvalov and his family. Meanwhile the onset of war and the involvement of Russian troops against Prussia in 1757 meant it was impossible for Hanbury-Williams to stay at court, and to Catherine's dismay he left. Poniatowski, too, was recalled to Poland for a while, though he returned in December 1756 as Polish envoy. Nearly a year later, in 1757, Catherine gave birth to a daughter Anna

The Seven Years War (1756–63) was a global conflict, fought not just in Europe but in India and the Americas as well. On one side stood Great Britain, Prussia and Hanover, while on the other were France, Austria, Russia, Saxony, Sweden and eventually Spain. Russia's involvement indicated its emergence as a significant player in European politics and diplomacy and the effectiveness of its troops. Frederick II (the Great) of Prussia seemed to be facing defeat despite many initial victories but he was helped by the death of Empress Elizabeth at the end of 1761 and the accession of the Prussian-loving Peter III, who quickly made peace with Prussia.

Petrovna, who is assumed to have been the Polish aristocrat's child – and whom once again was removed from her almost immediately after the birth.

It was in such a politically-charged atmosphere that Catherine's great hopes for the future were nearly destroyed as her new ally Bestuzhev dramatically fell from power. The trigger had been the surprise decision by the Russian military commander General S F Apraksin to withdraw his forces in September 1757 despite having beaten the Prussians in battle. The reason was that his supply lines had become over-extended but news of his retreat had provoked dark rumours in St Petersburg of Prussian influence at play. It also coincided with the Empress having a stroke, though she soon recovered. The general was recalled and questioned about his conduct, during which he admitted corresponding with Catherine; their connection was that he was a friend of Bestuzhev. Thanks to scheming by his rivals this was enough to lead to the arrest of Bestuzhev and his family in 1758. The suspicion was that he had plotted to change the succession. Fortunately for both of them, the Count was able to burn any compromising correspondence with the Grand Duchess before his arrest and he had also been able to warn Catherine to do likewise. These papers included the statesman's compromising plan outlining a formal role for Catherine in government when Peter acceded to the throne. Though Bestuzhev was never formally charged he was stripped of rank and sent into internal exile.

A black cloud now hung over Catherine, who had no powerful allies left at court. Peter had already privately questioned whether he was the father of Catherine's daughter Anna and now there was the suspicion that the Grand Duchess may somehow have become entangled in treasonable activities. The situation looked bleak. However, she kept her nerve and used the experience she had gleaned in 14 years at court in how to handle the angry Empress. At a tearful nighttime meeting, at which Peter was also present,

Catherine begged to be allowed to return to her home. She said she knew her children would be safe in Elizabeth's hands – all the time knowing that the Empress was extremely unlikely to agree to this embarrassing public split. The Grand Duchess also denied all suggestions of treason, pointing out that she had only written to General Apraksin as a friend, and had simply urged him to follow his orders. (Bestuzhev had shrewdly got Catherine to write such a letter the previous autumn.) She also defended herself against Peter's personal attacks on her, while the Grand Duke's own ranting against his wife served only to irritate the Empress.

After the interview was over, Peter still held out hopes that he would be allowed to get rid of Catherine and marry his mistress Elizabeth Vorontsova, who was the niece of the Vice-Chancellor. It was, however, just another sign of how little he understood either people or politics. Though the Empress may have been dismayed by some of Catherine's behaviour in the affair, she had respect for her – unlike her nephew whom according to Catherine she branded an 'idiot'. At a second meeting with the Empress a month later – this time alone – Catherine again protested her innocence and gradually the Grand Duchess was rehabilitated into court life. It is possible that Elizabeth – who shared Catherine's low opinions of Peter's likely merits as an emperor – may even have started to consider naming Paul as her heir, with Catherine as regent.[22]

Yet though she had survived the crisis, Catherine's position was still full of potential danger. The Empress' health was fading and despite Elizabeth's concerns, Peter was still set to be the next emperor. He, meanwhile, had now made it clear that he wanted a different woman to be his empress. Catherine was also hit by the sudden death of her daughter Anna in March 1759 and then saddened a year later by the death of her mother in Paris (who fortunately had disposed of any compromising letters Catherine had written to her.) As for her lover Poniatowski, he had returned to

Poland in mid-1758. By the end of the decade Catherine felt very alone and vulnerable. She desperately needed new and powerful allies if she was to fulfil her great dream – that of becoming Empress of All the Russias.

Becoming Empress 1760–2

Catherine's shrewd judgement of character led her to assume correctly that while the Empress shared her misgivings about Peter, she was unlikely to do anything about removing him from the succession. She noted that as the Empress was *slow in taking any decisions, particularly in her last years, one can guess that she also hesitated on the question of succession.*[23] Therefore if she wanted to survive, the Grand Duchess would need to draw upon her knowledge of court life, her ability to network, plus her own intelligence and considerable feminine charms. Otherwise she would be soon be at the mercy of a husband who seemed determined to jettison her at the first chance he had.

Peter, meanwhile, was still busy upsetting the Russian court. When an important Prussian prisoner of war, Count Schwerin, was brought to St Petersburg Grand Duke Peter feted him and made it clear that were he emperor he would release him. The Grand Duchess understood that this attitude did not much endear Peter to patriotic Russian nobles and officials. However, Catherine was soon just as interested in one of the young Guards officers whose job it had been to escort the Prussian count to St Petersburg. His name was Grigory Orlov, a Lieutenant in the Izmailovskii Guards who was already known for his bravery in battle, and who was considered the most handsome of the five Orlov brothers.

Catherine's passionate affair with Orlov – which probably began sometime in 1761 – was a happy coincidence of personal and political needs on her part. Emotionally she had been alone since the departure of Poniatowski and she quickly fell for Orlov's looks, his imposing physique, his bluff good humour and his natural air of authority and strength. Politically the relationship meant that Catherine quickly acquired a whole new network among the Guards, young, deeply patriotic Russians who were close to the centre of power and who potentially had the means to make or break emperors. However, Catherine prudently kept the affair with Orlov a secret even from some of her other close allies at the time.

The five Orlov brothers, Ivan, Alexei, Grigory, Fedor and Vladimir, were the sons of a provincial governor, and had a reputation for enjoying life to the full. They took part in bear hunting and cock fighting and were pugnacious by nature. The most talented soldier and most feared of the brothers was Alexei (who like Grigory was tall and powerfully built). The fourth brother Fedor was also a distinguished military figure. Between them, thanks to Grigory's position as Catherine's favourite, the Orlovs held considerable influence in the imperial court. Even after Grigory's fall as favourite Catherine continued to make use of their military and administrative services.

Catherine's forging of new alliances in the changed world of the court was not restricted to the Guards, important though they were. As early as 1756 she had discussed with her old friend Sir Charles Hanbury-Williams the potential of an emerging Russian diplomat by the name of Nikita Panin, someone she thought might make a future vice-chancellor (this was another sign of how she had been preparing for government in those uncertain years). Panin had been put in charge of young Paul's supervision and Catherine carefully and quietly cultivated him. A one-time protégé of Bestuzhev, Panin had been promoted thanks to Chancellor Vorontsov, but was neither in his camp nor in that of the other powerful court faction the Shuvalovs. Panin saw Catherine more as a potential regent for her son Paul than an empress in her own right. The cultivated and educated diplomat

Soldier and protector, Grigory Orlov, was the Empress's most influential lover. Both he and his family assisted her seizure of the throne of Russia

also wanted to move Russia gradually towards a more constitutional form of monarchy. However, his concern over Peter's aptitude for the throne still made Panin a useful ally. The Grand Duchess also made a useful friend in the form of Princess Ekaterina Dashkova, who happened to be the sister of Peter's mistress. The lively and intelligent princess felt more at home with the cultivated Catherine than with her sister and Peter, and the Grand Duchess was able to exploit her as a source of information.

By the end of 1761, therefore, as Elizabeth's reign drew to a close, Catherine had built up a diverse and powerful network of allies at court. However, her relationship with Orlov did produce one unforeseen disadvantage. For when the Empress finally died at the end of the year Catherine was already heavily pregnant by her lover. This fact alone guaranteed that the Grand Duchess could make no attempt to seize power from her husband Peter. Very few people knew of Catherine's pregnancy – she somehow managed to conceal it by the outfits she wore – and she knew that it had to be kept a secret. Trying to depose her husband when she was pregnant – whether people assumed it was his or a lover's – would look awful in the eyes of the world, quite apart from the practical consideration of taking such action while in that condition. It did not help matters either that Catherine was heavily in debt at the time. The excitable Princess Dashkova – who did not know of the pregnancy – apparently proposed a coup attempt involving her Guards officer husband as soon as Elizabeth died. However Catherine says that she immediately quashed such talk, describing it as *premature and immature*.[24]

The result was that Catherine, like everyone else at the Russian court, acquiesced in the accession of her husband and the Grand Duke was swiftly proclaimed Peter III. Significantly, there was no mention of Catherine or even his son Paul in the official proclamation. Catherine carried out her mourning for Elizabeth with conspicuous devotion – something she knew would please the Russian people – and took advantage of the voluminous black outfits to mask her condition. Her conduct was in strict contrast to that of the new Emperor who once again showed a remarkable lack of awareness of how his actions affected others. Peter made only the minimum effort to mourn the death of Elizabeth. Moreover, according to Catherine, the Emperor played a childish joke on his courtiers at the late Empress's funeral in late January by alternating his speed as he followed the hearse, causing them to drop his black train that they were carrying. She wrote later that *criticism of the Emperor's outrageous behaviour spread rapidly and his unsuitable deportment was the subject of much talk.*[25]

After the funeral Catherine effectively retired from court life so that she could get ready to have her child. The fact that relations between Peter and her had almost completely broken down probably helped smooth over her absence from court at this time. On 10 April 1762 she gave birth to Orlov's son, who was named Alexei Grigoryvich, and very quickly re-entered public life. On 21 April, for example, her 33rd birthday, she met with the ambassador from Austria. One of the reasons why she was quickly back into court life was that she knew that matters would soon come to a head. For this she had to thank her own husband, whose growing unpopularity and gift for upsetting people was beginning to reap its own rewards.

By no means all the measures that Peter III introduced in the early months of 1762 were bad or even all unpopular. The new Emperor had quickly abolished the loathed and feared Secret Chancery, the body charged with investigating supposed crimes against the state – investigations often conducted quite indiscriminately – and a precursor to the later NKVD and KGB. Though this did not mean the end of all state security operations, this move was widely popular. Just before this Peter III had also issued a manifesto freeing the nobility from compulsory service to the state in peacetime. Again, this was popular with much of the nobility, even though in practice most of them continued to work for the state because they relied on state patronage to flourish or at least survive. Some, though, feared the measure would reduce their influence. This reform was an attempt by the young Emperor to develop a professional bureaucracy separate from the aristocracy and one which would both provide and demand higher standards of administration.[26]

However, other measures announced by Peter helped alienate two of the most crucial and powerful forces in 18th-century Russia – the military and the Orthodox Church. First, the German-born Emperor alienated the church hierarchy by his obvious preference for Lutheranism and his disdain for the Russian liturgy. He then compounded this with going ahead with plans to secularise lands owned by monasteries.

Even more significantly, his foreign policy infuriated Russia's military officers. Early in 1762 Prussia had seemed on the brink of losing the Seven Years War after Russia's underrated forces had defeated its much-vaunted troops. Yet not only did the new Emperor immediately withdraw his troops, he also sued for peace with Prussia and his hero Frederick the Great. Indeed, Peter did not even demand East Prussia in return for a peace agreement, something that Frederick had been willing to concede. The new Emperor also envisaged going to war with Denmark, and fighting against her and Austria in alliance with Prussia. On top of this Peter III introduced Prussian drill and uniforms into the Russian army. This was a profound insult to the Russian army, especially as they had performed well against the Prussians. At the same time Peter began to rely on a small group of advisers, some of them German. They included Prince Georg-Ludwig, who was both Peter's and Catherine's uncle – he was the man who had proposed to her all those years ago when she was just 14.

Exactly when precise plans to launch a coup were drawn up is unclear. But it was soon obvious to Catherine and her supporters that they could not afford to delay for long. Peter's attitude towards his wife was graphically illustrated at a dinner to celebrate the peace treaty with Prussia. The Emperor used the opportunity of a silly dispute over imperial protocol to call his wife a fool in front of foreign dignitaries. Catherine cried then composed herself, but Peter had not finished with her. Later that evening he ordered an aide to have his wife arrested but fortunately the aide went instead to Prince Georg-Ludwig who managed to change the Emperor's mind. Such behaviour helped force the hand of the various plotters and by the middle of June at the latest plans were being drawn up to depose the Emperor. They knew that next time he might not change his mind.

It appears that the original aim was to wait until Peter left to lead the planned campaign against Denmark and arrest him as he went. (Frederick the Great had in fact warned his new ally against leaving the country in case he was deposed in his absence.) The main conspirators at this time appear to have been the Orlovs, the head of the Ukrainian Cossacks Count Kirill Razumovskii – brother of the late Elizabeth's old favourite and once in love with Catherine – Nikita Panin, Princess Dashkova, a leading official Grigory Teplov and a number of Guards officers. Catherine herself seems to have been at the heart of this web of conspiracy and worked closely with them, especially with the Orlov brothers – though Grigory was cautious as he feared he was being watched. By no means all the plotters shared precisely the same objectives. It was clear that Panin, for one, envisaged that Catherine would be installed as regent for Paul, and Princess Dashkova seems to have expected the same. Others such as the Orlovs – and certainly Catherine herself – sought nothing less than her proclamation as sovereign empress in her own right. However for now they were all united in the need for one thing – to overthrow Peter as quickly as possible.

Despite attempts at secrecy, rumours of an imminent coup were now rife in much of St Petersburg. It appears that even Peter himself heard of them but did nothing. One possible reason for the lack of action taken against the plotters was the fact that the German chief of police in the capital, Baron Korf, discreetly turned a blind eye to such talk. Once close to the Emperor, he had recently fallen out with him, and had meanwhile been quietly cultivated by Catherine. Yet nonetheless the conspirators were force to change their plans when on 27 June one of their senior members, Lieutenant Passek, was finally arrested after careless talk by a soldier. The time for action had arrived.

That day Catherine had been staying at the palace of Monplaisir at Petershof on the Gulf of Finland, just east of Oranienbaum where Peter was staying with his mistress. At dawn the following day Alexei Orlov, the scar-faced brother of Grigory, arrived at the palace unannounced with an urgent message for the slumbering Catherine. He told her that everything had been made ready for her proclamation, and that because of Passek's arrest they had to move at once. Catherine quickly dressed and she and Alexei left by a back entrance and headed immediately for St Petersburg. The suddenness of her departure meant that Catherine had not even had time to arrange her hair, though fortunately (and curiously) their carriage met with her hairdresser travelling in the opposite direction and he was able to see to her hair. Now suitably coiffured, she and Alexei sped off for her meeting with destiny.

Shortly before she arrived at the capital she met her lover Grigory who had fresh horses to help the small party on the final part of its journey. By 8 a.m. Catherine had reached her first important destination— the quarters of the Izmailovskii Guards. Here, amid emotional scenes, the colonel-in-chief of the regiment Count Kirill Razumovskii led the officers and men in swearing allegiance to the new Empress – their 'Little Mother' as they called her. Soon the soldiers from other barracks joined suit, with the men of the Preobrazhenskii Guards apologising for their delay, saying that they had had to arrest some of their officers who had remained loyal to Peter. Troops from the Old Imperial Guard – who to their disgust had been disbanded by Peter – joined the growing crowds while many soldiers now pointedly donned their old Russian uniforms rather than the new and despised Prussian-style ones. Catherine later described the scenes as a *frenzy of joy*.[27]

Events were now moving quickly and Catherine was taken by the

It was from the Monplaisir Palace on the Gulf of Finland that Catherine, and the Orlovs, launched her seizure of the throne of Russia

Orlovs and other Guards through the growing and excited crowds to the Church of Our Lady of Kazan – where she had married Peter back in 1745 – to be greeted by the Archbishop of Novgorod. Here she was proclaimed Empress of All the Russias and prayers were offered for the new Catherine the Second. By 10 a.m. Catherine had made her way triumphantly to the Winter Palace where yet more officials swore oaths of allegiance. Then Panin brought his young charge Paul to the palace and the child was rapturously greeted by the crowds when he appeared with his mother on the balcony. However, though Paul was named as the new Empress' successor in the official proclamation – prepared some days before by Catherine herself – there was no mention of her ruling in Paul's name. Through their swift action Catherine and the Orlovs had got their way. Panin and others who had wanted a regency had been out-manoeuvred by the sheer speed of the coup. Reluctantly they now had to acquiesce in Catherine's dramatic rise to power. Meanwhile a pre-written manifesto proclaimed the reasons for the new Empress's assumption of power, and it was unashamedly and astutely patriotic in tone. The German-born Empress said that the Orthodox Church had been in peril, that the country's military reputation had been tarnished and that the empire's institutions were under threat. *Therefore ... We were compelled ... to mount our all-Russian sovereign throne*, the manifesto loftily concluded.[28]

Amid all the euphoria, it was not forgotten that the empire already had a lawfully-enthroned emperor, the hapless Peter III who was still at Oranienbaum. Catherine now demonstrated how well she understood that all monarchies, including the Russian one, thrive on strong images. Not content with sending troops to arrest her husband, the new Empress borrowed a uniform of the Preobrazhenskii Guards, leapt on a grey stallion named Brilliant and, sabre in hand, led a force of more than 10,000 troops westwards out of the city. Catherine, who had made herself a colonel of the regiment – the same rank taken by Peter the Great – was an excellent horsewoman and knew that she cut a fine figure in her uniform. She knew that the powerful image she was creating would linger in people's minds for a long time. Together with her senior officers Catherine rode off to huge acclaim.

While Catherine had been busily seizing power, her husband had cut an increasingly forlorn figure. Peter, his mistress and courtiers had travelled to Petershof on the 28th where they had been expecting to dine with Catherine to celebrate his name day the following day. Though he appears to have been informed during the short journey of the dramatic events in the capital, this did not stop him searching high and low for his wife at Monplaisir. He is reported to have searched wardrobes and even under the bed for her. It was as if at the very time Catherine was marching towards her destiny as empress, Peter was retreating into childishness as he faced the end of his brief reign.

Three of Peter's senior officials – Prince Trubetskoy and counts Shuvalov and Vorontsov – hurried to St Petersburg, apparently to try to thwart Catherine in whatever plans she had. But of the three, only Vorontsov refused to swear allegiance immediately to Catherine. Peter, his court now in disarray, chose to head for the island fortress of Kronstadt. At around midnight the Emperor, who as usual had been drinking, and his nervous entourage made their way in a yacht towards the fortress and what they hoped was safety. However, they had arrived too late. Admiral Talyzin from St Petersburg had already taken control of Kronstadt in Catherine's name. When Peter's yacht finally arrived and the Emperor himself yelled at a sentry demanding entry, he was told that Peter III no longer existed – and that moreover if the vessel did not turn round, it would be fired on. Peter seems to have been broken by this hammer blow. He returned meekly to Oranienbaum where Alexei Orlov, who had been leading an advance party of troops, was easily able to take control. In Frederick the Great's famous phrase, Peter had 'let himself be driven from the throne as a child is sent to bed'.[29]

The unfortunate Peter sent two plaintive notes to Catherine, who was still making her way to Petershof. The first sought to negotiate with his wife, while accepting his faults, while in the second Peter renounced his throne and pleaded to be allowed to return to Holstein. However Catherine was interested only in Peter's formal abdication. When she arrived in style at Petershof she received an abdication letter that had now been signed by the distraught Peter. The former emperor then arrived at Petershof but Catherine spared herself and him the ordeal of seeing him. He was later taken to his estate at Ropsha, pending his departure for rather more secure accommodation at the island fortress of Schlüsselburg. He was never to make it that far.

The official reason for Peter's death days later on 6 July 1762 was that he had suffered a severe attack of 'haemorrhoidal colic'

The Proclamation of the reign of Empress Catherine II is announced in
St Petersburg

though understandably this explanation was greeted with incre-
dulity, especially outside Russia. The deposed emperor had been
in the care of Alexei Orlov and other soldiers and there can be
little doubt that he was murdered. From the point of view of the
Orlov clan there was a good reason for removing Peter. His death
made Catherine a widow and meant that – legally if not necess-
sarily politically – she was free to marry Grigory Orlov. From
Catherine's perspective the death got rid of someone who, despite
his unpopularity, could always have served as a rallying point
for the disaffected. After all, he was a direct descendent of Peter
the Great. This did not mean, however, that she had ordered his
murder. What seems likely is that she probably understood that
her husband's death was inevitable but had played no direct part
in sanctioning it. Certainly there was no question of a criminal
investigation into Peter's death for 'haemorrhoids'. A letter from
Alexei Orlov in which he admitted that Peter was killed during

a drunken row and for which he accepted ultimate responsibility and begged her forgiveness was locked away until her death. It was not made public until the late 19th century and certainly suggests she had not ordered her husband's murder.[30]

After years of careful observation of the Russian scene from the inside, Catherine was determined not to repeat the mistakes of some of her predecessors. In particular she was keen to make sure that powerful figures who had served previous rulers did not now feel alienated and become potential sources of opposition. Therefore Catherine kept on Count Vorontsov as her Chancellor, despite his initial reluctance to swear allegiance to her, though the importance of his post diminished. Ivan Shuvalov was also not banished and even Peter III's mistress Elizabeth Vorontsova was later set up in a house in Moscow, on condition she refrained from meddling in court affairs. Throughout her reign Catherine was generally more inclined to win over people by favours than by banishing or punishing them.

As for her supporters, the Empress was to prove very generous, both now and in the future, and showered money, estates and serfs, as well as bestowing titles and posts in Russia's unique social hierarchy.

The Table of Ranks was established by Peter the Great in 1722 and was a system of military, civil service and court hierarchy. There were 14 different ranks, with number fourteen at the bottom and number one at the top. Each rank had its corresponding position in the civil service, army and navy; for example rank 12 would be a provincial secretary in the civil service, a second lieutenant in the army and a midshipman in the navy. Anyone attaining rank eight in the civil service became a hereditary noble, while anyone at rank 14 in the military automatically got this privilege – and with it the right to own serfs. The effect of the table was to value service rank above social position.

Indeed Catherine handed out more than a million roubles-worth of cash and serfs in all to her fellow plotters including 24,000 roubles (or 800 serfs) each to Grigory and Alexei Orlov, and Lieutenant Peter Passek, while Panin and Razumovskii each received a lifetime pension of 5,000 roubles a year. Meanwhile the loyal soldiers of St Petersburg received between them a total of more than 225,000 roubles. Catherine rarely if ever neglected her friends and supporters.

Almost immediately, also, the new Empress set about arranging a lavish coronation, which tradition dictated had to be in the old capital, Moscow. Peter, with his typically scorn for most things Russian, had not even bothered to arrange one. Catherine however wanted to prove to her subjects that she was proud to be Empress of Russia and was determined to cement her position by being formally crowned in front of her people. After all, given that she was a German princess with no blood claim to the Russian throne, she knew that she had to work hard to demonstrate her fitness to reign. Now all that remained was to start trying to work out how to rule this vast, unwieldy and still largely backward empire. At least it was a task for which she had assiduously prepared herself.

A Desire for Change 1762–8

Catherine's splendid and expensive coronation took place in the Assumption Cathedral in the Kremlin on Sunday 22 September 1762. Catherine had ordered a jewel-encrusted crown for the occasion and this she placed on her own head during the ceremony as cannons boomed outside. It was a remarkable moment for a woman who at 33 was in her prime but who nonetheless had no legal claim whatsoever to be Empress of All the Russias.

The precariousness of Catherine's position was in fact apparent even as she placed the crown on her head. A notable absentee from the ceremony was her eight-year-old son and heir Paul who was poorly. The boy had been quite a sickly child from birth – Catherine partly blamed this on the old-fashioned way in which Elizabeth had insisted he be brought up – and ill-health would continue to dog his childhood. His poor health was not just a concern for Catherine as a mother but also as empress. Paul was – at least as far as the outside world knew – a direct descendant of Peter the Great and therefore a legitimate heir. While he lived even those who did not approve of her ruling in her own right could tolerate Catherine being empress until Paul was old enough to take over the reins of government. In a sense he was a kind of constitutional fig-leaf to cover her own embarrassing lack of legitimacy. If, however, the sickly Paul died, then her lack of legal entitlement to the imperial throne would be terribly exposed.

For her part, Catherine never for a second considered herself as

Empress Catherine II in her coronation regalia

a temporary empress and from the start she intended to govern her adopted country as absolute and unchallenged monarch. It was a task for which she had prepared herself. During those long and often precarious years at court as Grand Duchess, Catherine had learnt about governance and diplomacy through her husband's dealings with Holstein, and through her contacts with tutors in the dark arts of politics and diplomacy such as Hanbury-Williams and also Count Bestuzhev, who was now recalled from exile and restored to favour. She had also set out to develop her own theories of governing through her reading and prodigious correspondence. She read the works of Voltaire – with whom she would now correspond for many years – and Montesquieu and the *Encyclopaedia* of the French philosopher Denis Diderot. Though she was no intellectual, Catherine was intelligent, well read and genuinely interested in the theory of government. She had thought hard about the problems of ruling an empire as vast as Russia. This was the Age of the Enlightenment in Western Europe and Catherine was in many ways a child of the Enlightenment. She shared many of the Enlightenment values of truth, justice, and the desire for modern and efficient government, and planned to apply many of these ideas to Russia. Catherine saw herself as a philosopher queen.

But despite this, Catherine was very firm in her views about the need for a strong ruler to govern Russia. At no point did she even flirt with the idea of reducing the autocratic and technically absolute powers of the Russian crown. Nor did she ever consider even a limited form of elected assembly that could take part in the government of the country. For her, good government in Russia meant an enlightened but all-powerful emperor/empress who could reform and manage the Russian state to the

Voltaire was the pen name of François-Marie Arouet (1694–1778), the French writer, essayist and proponent of the rights of man and a trenchant critic of the Church. From 1763 he and Catherine II corresponded regularly in a kind of mutual appreciation society. From her point of view the friendship and support of a leading figure in the Enlightenment greatly enhanced her status as an enlightened ruler. Charles-Louis de Secondat Montesquieu (1689–1755) was another key figure in the Enlightenment and Catherine drew heavily on his most important work *The Spirit of the Laws*, published in 1748, for her Great Instruction. Montesquieu extolled the virtue of moderate monarchies where there was a separation of powers and criticised Asiatic 'despotisms'.

benefit of all its peoples. Throughout her reign Catherine would trust in and rely on some very able advisors and administrators – one of her main gifts lay in spotting such people – but she always demanded that ultimate authority lay with her.

This resolute belief in undiluted power at the top was shown early when Catherine rejected a plan from Nikita Panin for a new imperial council to help govern Russia. The idea was that Catherine would be able to choose the members of the council – but could not then dismiss them once they had been appointed. By now the wily Panin was an important figure who had control over Paul's upbringing and had backed Catherine's coup, and the plan was given serious consideration. But given its clear shackles on her power to hire and fire officials – and the fact it was opposed by the Orlovs – it is hardly surprising the council was never established.

Instead Catherine had her own ideas for the need to reform Russia's ramshackle administration and legal system. Initially these included the appointment of key officials who could be relied upon to carry out her wishes and to offer good and honest advice. One key appointment was that of Prince Alexander Viazemskii as Procurator General, an important position that in Catherine's reign effectively combined the roles of prime minister, home secretary, attorney general and finance minister. Viazemskii was to prove a loyal and shrewd administrator throughout much of Catherine's long reign. A good idea of Catherine's attention to detail, her hands on approach to government and also her attitude towards her advisers are contained in instructions she wrote to Viazemskii on how to handle both the senate and also what she expected from him. She wrote: *If I see that you are loyal, hard-working, open and sincere, then you can be assured of my unbounded confidence. Above all I love the truth, and you must feel to say it without fear; you can argue with me without danger, provided that the end result is good ... I do not require flattery from you, but only sincerity and a firm attitude towards business.*[31]

Her reference to a *firm attitude towards business* was typical of Catherine who was herself hardworking and expected those around her to show the same application. This hands-on approach to government came as something of a shock to some of the old court officials who had got used to life under the rather less diligent Elizabeth. However, to those officials who worked hard and stayed loyal to Catherine, she invariably showed great kindness over the years. The Empress also established her own working routine, which involved getting up early, lighting her own fire and making her own black coffee, after which she would start writing. Later in the morning she would see officials to discuss government business. Though Catherine was at home in the formal surroundings of the court and cut an impressive figure at such gatherings all her life, in her everyday routine she favoured informality and simplicity.

One of Catherine's early reforms was of the Senate, a judicial and administrative body, whose sessions she attended. She was less than impressed with the poor time-keeping of many members and of the quality of their discussion. Part of the effect of the reform, which divided the Senate into six departments, was to put more power into the hands of the procurator general. Another sign of Catherine's thoughtful approach to government was shown when Michael Vorontsov finally vacated the post of Chancellor. He was never formally replaced and in a sense there was no need – for Catherine effectively performed the role herself.

Apart from the desire to reform Russia's creaking bureaucracy, Catherine faced other pressing problems. One concerned both her private life and her public status – the question of whether she should re-marry. The Orlovs were naturally keen for Catherine's favourite Grigory to marry the Empress, something that would cement their already powerful position in imperial Russia. Yet the idea that Catherine should marry a soldier such as Orlov was anathema to many at court, including her supporters. Panin perhaps spoke for many when he is reported to have said that 'a Madame Orlova could never be empress of all the Russias'.[32] Later, in the spring of 1763, Catherine had the ageing Bestuzhev circulate a paper seeking the support of officials for the idea of her remarrying. However, all this achieved was lots of wild rumours and an outburst by one of the officers who helped in her coup, Fedor Khitrovo, criticising the power of the Orlovs. He was later arrested and banished to his estates for his bitter remarks. But Catherine was above all a realist and she now realised the depth of opposition her re-marriage could provoke. The bluff and relatively unsophisticated Orlov would have to be content with remaining simply the Empress' favourite.

In foreign affairs the cautious Panin gradually became the dominant character in Catherine's government, even though the Empress was always the main driver of policy. When she had seized power Catherine had immediately cancelled Peter III's plans for an attack on Denmark and rejected the idea of a formal alliance with Prussia, one of the policies that had made Peter so unpopular. However she did not want to alienate Frederick the Great as they had a common interest in Poland, a country badly weakened by her neighbours during the Seven Years War. Instead a chance arose for Catherine to meddle in Polish affairs when in the autumn of 1763 the Polish king Augustus III died. Catherine knew just the person whom she wanted to become king – Polish monarchs were elected – and that was her former lover Stanislas Poniatowski. Poniatowski had for some time still harboured hopes that there was a place for him in Catherine's life, an idea that did not remotely fit in with her plans. Instead she wanted the Polish nobleman on the throne of Poland where she felt that he could be of use to her. And indeed, with the 'protection' of Russian troops to make sure the result went the right way, Poland's Election Diet duly elected Poniatowski, who took the title Stanislas II. It would not be the last time that Catherine would intervene in Polish affairs.

A satirical print showing the partition of Poland between Catherine of Russia, Joseph II of Austria and Frederick the Great of Prussia in 1773

Catherine was always very wary about any hint of plots against her, especially if they involved members of the Guards. She had, after all, seized the throne herself largely thanks to young officers. A very early scare had occurred days after her coronation when she was informed of a conspiracy among members of the Izmailovskii Guards in Moscow. In reality it appears to have involved little more than drunken threats during a dinner. However what really alarmed Catherine was that the 'conspiracy' had apparently discussed the installation of the imprisoned Ivan VI as emperor – he had been deposed as a child by Elizabeth and kept secretly as a prisoner at Schlüsselburg ever since. Catherine was both angry and worried by this link between Guardsmen and Ivan, though death sentences passed on the lead plotters were characteristically commuted to loss of rank and exile to Siberia.

Far more serious, if ultimately doomed, was the plot that took place in July 1764, while Catherine was visiting the Baltic provinces. The chief protagonist was a Ukrainian officer, Lieutenant Vasilii Mirovich, who had learnt the true identity of the mysterious and nameless 'prisoner number one' at Schlüsselburg. His plan was to set Ivan free and take him to St Petersburg where he would be proclaimed emperor. Mirovich's plan was nearly ruined before it had begun when his chief fellow conspirator was drowned, but the officer, who was the son of an exiled Ukrainian nobleman and who was fixated on restoring the family's fortune, forged ahead regardless. Supported by his troops Mirovich burst into the fortress late at night in dense fog and knocked the commandant senseless. However, what the young officer did not know was that Ivan's two guards had been under longstanding orders – reconfirmed by Catherine – that if ever an attempt was made to free Ivan they were immediately to kill the former emperor. The two guards followed their orders to the letter and when Mirovich asked to see Ivan he was shown the young man's body lying in a pool of blood. Realising there was no point in continuing, the rebel officer gave himself up.

Catherine was naturally alarmed at the news of the plot and yet also strangely relieved at Ivan's death; Ivan after all was always likely to be a potential rallying point for the disaffected and now he was gone. *God's guidance is miraculous and unfathomable,* was her reaction, though she cut short her brief excursion to Mitau in Kurland (now Jelgava in Latvia) – incidentally the only time that Catherine left her empire during her reign.[33] Mirovich himself was beheaded and some of the soldiers who followed him were given savage floggings. Though Mirovich's venture was doomed to failure, and involved no widespread conspiracy, it was yet another reminder of Catherine's own lack of legitimacy. And though it had ultimately removed a second potential rival to the throne, that too had come at a cost. The deaths of Peter and Ivan were stains on Catherine's reputation, especially in Europe. This mattered not just politically but personally too for a woman who would become increasingly anxious about her historical legacy. The supposed murder of two rivals hardly increased her credentials to be an enlightened philosopher-ruler.

However, Catherine's image as a reforming empress were enhanced by a major project of the mid-1760s that made clearer her vision for Russia. The Empress had already shown her willingness to modernise and secularise the empire when in 1764 she brought church lands and serfs under state control. It was a policy originally proposed by Peter III but his open disdain towards the Orthodox Church made it even harder for the hierarchy to accept. Under Catherine, however, who had always been careful to follow the customs of the church diligently and who was generally sympathetic towards it, there was little real opposition from the church. Catherine stamped her authority on the church and showed where real political power lay, but she was not threatening the church's central role in Russian life. One senior cleric, Metropolitan Arsenii

early drafts that seemed to hint at its abolition one day were removed.

Catherine's 'Great Instruction' was not intended to exist in a political vacuum and her idea was that it would be a practical guide for Russian lawmakers in a bid to codify the country's shambolic system of laws. To this end she announced late in 1766 that a special body would meet in Moscow the following year and whose stated aim would be to carry out this codification and reform. The so-called Legislative Commission was to be composed of the nobility, townsfolk, free peasants and Cossacks. These were also to bring with them a list of instructions or *nakaz* about what changes in the law they might wish. This commission was in no way an assembly or parliament and did not imply any desire on Catherine's part to share power. However it was intended to show that she wanted the people's (or at least a section of it) involvement in the better governing of the country. Catherine herself planned to open the Commission at which time her own Great Instruction would take centre stage.

Before the Commission was scheduled to meet, Catherine decided to set off on a trip down the River Volga far to the east of Moscow and far away both in distance and in culture from the rather more Westernised Russia to which she had become used. One of the reasons for undertaking the trip was so that she could see another side of the empire she ruled. Another reason was that she knew such a high profile journey – among her 2,000-strong entourage were diplomats from across Europe – would enhance her reputation internationally as a dynamic and bold leader. For example, in March 1767 on the eve of the journey she wrote rather consciously to her regular correspondent Voltaire that *when you least expect it you will receive a letter from some remote corner of Asia*. Catherine knew that such public correspondence would reach a much wider audience.[36]

Catherine and her entourage – which included Grigory Orlov,

though her son Paul stayed in Moscow – left that city at the end of April and returned in mid-June. During that time she voyaged onboard the galley *Tver* and saw numerous towns and people along the way. She visited ancient monasteries, was warmly received by crowds and noted with interest the fertility of much of that region. Catherine was especially struck by the town of Kazan which displayed both wealth and a cultural and ethnic diversity that made an impression on her. The lessons of this trip were not lost on her and her attempts to improve the government of the empire. Catherine wrote to Voltaire about the *difference of climate, peoples, customs and even ideas!... There are in this city twenty different peoples, which in no way resemble one another. We have nevertheless to design a garment to fit them all.*[37] Her main frustration in what was for her a fascinating and enlightening trip was that it slowed down correspondence and meant that she sometimes felt out of touch with news; Catherine always loved to know exactly what was going on around her.

On her return to Moscow – a city she had disliked since her first stay in 1744 – Catherine prepared for the historic start of her legislative Commission. This took place on 30 July 1767 in the Kremlin when the Empress' greeting to the deputies included the claim that they had a unique chance to *glorify yourselves and your century, to acquire for yourselves the respect and gratitude of future centuries* ... The commission then began work with the reading of Catherine's 'Great Instruction' which took five sessions and was completed on 9 August. Shortly afterwards a group of deputies sought to get Catherine to accept the title of 'The Great, Most Wise, and Mother of the Fatherland', an honour she graciously and modestly declined. The opening of the commission certainly succeeded in getting Catherine talked about across Europe, even if some of the talk – as in later centuries – regarded the whole consultative exercise as little more than a public relations exercise. In fact if the Empress was guilty of anything it was probably naivety

An engraving of the Winter Palace and Falconet's statue of Peter the Great in St Petersburg

in thinking that Enlightenment ideals could simply be applied to Russia society and bring about rapid change. Most Russians, including many nobles, cared or knew nothing of theories of government and concentrated on rather more mundane, parochial issues.[38]

Away from lofty affairs of state, Catherine had some more cultural matters to attend to. The Empress had been privately scornful – not entirely justly – of the lack of culture that had permeated the Russian court under Elizabeth. Now that she was in power she was determined that Russia should be regarded as not just a great power militarily and diplomatically, but artistically and culturally too. Once again she understood the power of image; it was important that her court shone in all respects. In 1764 she bought more than 200 Old Master paintings from a Berlin dealer and from then on embarked on a lifelong collecting spree that was to form the basis of the renowned collection at the Hermitage in

St Petersburg. And though she had little ear for music herself, she also engaged the Italian composer and performer Baldassare Galuppi to come to the imperial court, while in 1766 she also commissioned the sculptor Etienne Maurice Falconet to produce a statue of Peter the Great. Yet another sign of her determination to be a renowned patron of arts and letters was her move to buy Denis Diderot's entire library when the French philosopher fell into financial difficulties.

Despite the court's growing international reputation and the generally favourable reception Catherine's Instruction and Commission had received, she still had concerns closer to home. The health of her son Paul continued to give cause for anxiety and this was heightened in 1768 when Panin's fiancée died of smallpox. Though she had been wary of doctors since childhood she was keen to ensure that neither she nor Paul succumbed to this virulent disease. As a result she took the bold decision that year to send for a British doctor by the name of Thomas Dimsdale to have both herself and her son inoculated against smallpox. Under conditions of secrecy the inoculations were carried out, and to the relief and gratitude of Catherine both she and Paul – plus Orlov too – came through the ordeal with no significant problems. With typical generosity the Empress awarded Dimsdale a lump sum in cash, an annual pension and made him a baron of the Russian Empire.

Apart from smallpox, however, there were other, more tangible threats looming on the horizon. Since seizing the throne, Catherine's Russia had been at peace, but now that was to change. Indeed the main work of her Legislative Commission had to be halted at the end of 1768 as war loomed, and it would never start again – though its work and that of the 'Great Instruction' would bear fruit later in her reign. For now though reform was largely put on hold as Catherine looked south at Russia's longstanding rival in that region – the Ottoman Empire.

Foreign Adventures 1768–71

Peter the Great's victories over the Swedes in the Great Northern War had given the empire crucial access to the Baltic Sea. By 1721 Peter was no longer simply the Tsar of Muscovy but was styled Emperor of All the Russias, and it was clear that the new empire was becoming a major military force in Europe. However, though he had tried to extend Russia's borders to the south, Peter had failed to defeat the Russians' traditional rivals in that region, the Ottoman Empire.

Catherine knew her Russian history well and understood that it was one of the cherished aims of the country that one day it would challenge the Turks for domination of the Black Sea, which at that time was essentially a Turkish lake. With all the zeal of a converted Russian patriot Catherine gradually began to eye the opportunities for military glory and territorial conquest in the south, with the twin aim of boosting the prestige both of Russia and herself. Ultimately she would harbour grandiose plans that envisaged the replacement of the Ottoman Empire in Europe with a new version of the long-defunct Byzantine Empire – her so-called Greek Project. However, Catherine was to find herself embroiled in conflict with the Turks rather sooner than she had perhaps imagined. This was as a result of some rather naïve and unsubtle meddling in Poland.

The Empress had inherited a common feeling among many Russians of disdain for Poland and its rather chaotic political system and also a mistrust of Catholicism, the dominant religion there. At the same time her early success in placing her former lover Poniatowski on the Polish throne in 1764 had made the Empress over-confident in her ability to influence foreign affairs. This was demonstrated in the rather gushing way that she congratulated Panin and herself on their success with the king *that we have made.* The result was that she overdid Russia's involvement in Poland over the following years, meddling on behalf of Polish dissidents — that is non-Catholics, who included Lutherans as well as Orthodox believers. Many Poles reacted defiantly against Russian interference and groups of opponents known as Confederates sprang up to defend their freedoms and traditions. Meanwhile the presence of so many of Catherine's troops in Poland to put down the rebellion unnerved other European powers notably France and her allies the Turks, whose own lands bordered on Polish territory.[39]

In the summer of 1768 this potentially explosive situation was detonated when a group of Ukrainian Cossacks who were pursuing Polish confederates kept on going over the border and sacked the town of Balta, which was under the control of the Khanate of the Crimea and a dependency of the Ottoman Empire. By the end of September the Turks had demanded the removal of all Russian troops from Poland. When the Russian envoy refused this demand

The Islamic Ottoman Empire, whose capital was Istanbul, had finally supplanted the old Byzantine Empire in 1453 and had extended her control through Greece, the Balkan states and up through what are today Romania, Bulgaria and Moldavia. The Turks dominated the Black Sea either indirectly or through their control of the Tatar khanate in the Crimea. Therefore the Ottoman Empire, which was in slow decline though still very powerful, stood between an emerging and expanding Russia and its access to the Black Sea and ultimately the Mediterranean. At the end of the 17th century Peter the Great had briefly seized Taganrog and Azov on the small Sea of Azov, east of the Crimea, but soon had to surrender them.

he was locked up in the fortress of the Seven Towers, the traditional Turkish way of declaring war. After six years of peace, Catherine II was finally at war.

Though Catherine had not actively sought war with the Ottoman Empire at this time, the declaration neither hugely surprised or dismayed her. By 1765 Catherine had approved some important reforms of the Russian military – which had already proved itself against the supposedly mighty Prussians – and its numbers had swelled to more than 300,000. It would increase by another 100,000 by the 1790s. At the same time the navy, established under Peter the Great, had also been increased in size and its officers sent for training overseas, while the recruitment of foreign officers, including many Britons, improved its know-how. Catherine now felt it was time to pursue Peter's frustrated dreams in the south.

War was a stop-start affair in the 18th century with serious fighting generally ceasing during the winter. This gave time for Catherine and her newly-formed war council a chance to make their plans. The Empress herself seemed invigorated by the challenge ahead. She was now 39 and though the first flush of youth had faded, and her slender figure had already started to stiffen and fill, in many ways she was in her physical as well as intellectual prime. William Richardson, tutor to the children of the British envoy Lord Cathcart, gave a detailed description of the Empress in August 1768 when she attended the laying of the foundation stone of the new St Isaac's Church. Richardson wrote that she was 'taller than the middle size, very comely, gracefully formed, but inclined to grow corpulent; and of a fair complexion, which like every other female in this country, she endeavours to improve by the addition of rouge. She has a fine mouth and teeth; and blue eyes, expressive of scrutiny, something not so good as observation, and not so bad as suspicion. Her features are in general regular and pleasing ... her demeanour to all around her seemed very smiling and courteous'.[40]

A portrait of Catherine the Great in middle age reveals the face of a matronly and serene woman

In her private life, too, Catherine was mostly content. She and Grigory Orlov had settled into a pattern of life that was almost like that of a married couple. The main difference was that Catherine was usually scrupulous about keeping a division between the personal and the political at court, and in public showed decorum and no undue signs of affection towards her favourite. Orlov did not share all of the Empress' intellectual interests and was not particularly well-read or especially cultured, but nonetheless he was good natured, good company, physically impressive and a reassuring presence in her life. Though she was careful not to promote Orlov beyond his abilities, and was also wary about arousing jealousies in other factions, she found him a surprisingly capable administrator on occasions. For example an early economic policy of the Empress was to encourage immigrants to come to Russia to help develop its sparsely-populated and expanding lands. Orlov was put in charge of this in 1763 and over the next ten years he oversaw the arrival of some 30,000 immigrants – many of them German – into Russia's southern territories.

Of course Orlov was also a soldier by profession, and in late 1767 it was he who came up with a plan of attack in the war against the Ottoman Empire that appealed to Catherine in its boldness and for the prospects that it opened up for Russia. His idea was to send a fleet all the way from the Baltic, down through the Straits of Gibraltar and to cross the Mediterranean and confront the Turkish fleet there. Though it was opposed by some of her war council, Catherine ultimately sanctioned this expensive but daring plan. Another idea was to encourage the non-Muslim peoples under Ottoman control – for example in Greece and the Dalmatian coast – to lend their support. Meanwhile in Russia itself serfs were called up for compulsory military service from their villages to take part in the impending campaign.

The war started well for Russia and Catherine was quickly buoyed by news of some modest Russian advances at Azov and Taganrog. Another victory, this time in July by Field Marshal Alexander Golitsyn, produced in Catherine the kind of exuberance that had greeted her initial success in Poland back in 1764.

A bust of Alexander Golitsyn. His successful military campaign in the Caucasus extended Russian territory towards the Black Sea

My soldiers are off to fight the Turks as if they were going to a wedding, she wrote exultantly to Voltaire, who thoroughly approved of his imperial friend's campaign against the Asiatic Ottoman Empire. *Wherever the Turks or the Tartars* [Muslim inhabitants of the Crimea] *show themselves, we send them away with a sound thrashing* ... There were more Russian advances to follow, and Catherine light-heartedly introduced herself to a Russian general as the *new Moldavian princess* in recognition of victories there later in the year.

Yet the impatient Empress was to discover that wars fought over large areas and hampered by slow lines of transport and communication were frustrating affairs, and she became worried at the lack of decisive breakthroughs.[41]

The industrious Catherine, however, was also preoccupied with other matters even as she fought her first war. Her growing interest in matters artistic – though she never claimed to have a great eye for art herself – was demonstrated when she acquired hundreds more works, many of them by Old Masters, in 1768 and 1769. She bought such works on the advice of an informal network of agents around Europe, who included Diderot, the philosopher, who had been grateful for the Empress' patronage.

Her fascination with cultural matters and with the nature of society coincided in early 1769 with her promotion of a new periodical in Russia – *Vsyakaya vsyachina* ('All sorts of things'). It was unusual enough for a ruler to support a new publication such as this in Russia; what is quite striking is that the purpose of this periodical, consciously modelled on British publications such as *Tatler* and *The Spectator*, was to poke gentle fun at Russian society. The inveterate writer Catherine – who was later to try her hands at writing history, librettos and plays – may even have contributed to the periodical. Though neither *Vsyakaya vsyachina* nor its rivals that soon sprang up lasted very long – there was a limited market at the time – they did have a galvanising effect both on Russian intellectual life and on society's ability to examine itself. The precise reasons why Catherine chose to get involved in this project – and at such a time – are unclear. Perhaps she saw it as the start of an attempt to educate her people and introduce them to the sophistication of Western cultural life.

The arrival of spring in 1770 meant that hostilities were resumed between the Russians and the Turks. Initially the news was far from promising for a frustrated Catherine, as first floods and then an outbreak of plague – a portent of what was to come rather later – hampered Russian progress. Suddenly, however, the news got dramatically better. First of all Catherine was informed of two major victories in land battles against the Turks and Tartars at Larga and then Kagul in July, under the leadership of General Rumiantsev. Catherine was delighted but soon afterwards even better news belatedly reached her of events that had happened some time earlier, on 24–26 June, in the Aegean Sea. She was informed that the Russians had smashed the Turkish fleet

The Russian navy's victory over the Turks at Chesme was an astonishing achievement. For one thing, the Turkish fleet was experienced and knew the waters well, while the Russian fleet, despite the presence of British officers such as Admiral Samuel Greig and Rear Admiral John Elphinstone, was still learning its trade. In addition the fleet had had to make its way all around the coast of Western Europe – the British helped by allowing it to put in at Hull and Portsmouth – before reaching the Mediterranean. Moreover the commander in charge of the Russian fleet was Alexei Orlov, a man of undoubted bravery and skill on the battlefield but with absolutely no experience of naval warfare. However, he had been convalescing in Italy at the time and Catherine had trusted him implicitly to lead the arriving Russian fleet. And indeed the Russians had prevailed, defeating the Turks in an encounter in open sea and then burning their fleet in harbour. In all the Turks were said to have lost 11,000 men.

The Empress rapturously greeted what was proclaimed as Russia's first naval victory in 900 years. As ever she wrote to Voltaire with her thoughts, knowing that this would result in her words being communicated to a wider European audience (though they seemed spontaneous the letters were carefully drafted before the final version was written). *They say that the earth and sea trembled with the huge number of exploding ships ... War is a wretched business sir! Count Orlov tells me that the water of the harbour of Chesme, which is not very large, was stained with blood, so many Turks had perished there.*

The influence of the Italian Baroque architects can be seen in Rastrelli's Grotto, on the Great Pond in the Catherine Park near St Petersburg

For his part Voltaire likened her victories to those of Hannibal and described Catherine as the 'avenger of Europe'.[42] Catherine showered honours around for the heroes of Chesme and other battles. Alexei Orlov was allowed the honour of adding Chesmenskii to his name after the place where the battle was won, *Te Deums* were sung and a memorial to Peter the Great – the founder of the navy – was held. Rumiantsev was meanwhile made a field marshal.

Catherine also erected monuments to each victory in the grounds of Tsarkoye Selo. This royal complex – which literally means 'Tsar's village' and which lies 16 miles south of St Petersburg – was the Empress' favourite palace and was somewhere where she could genuinely relax. It was here, during her breaks from following events in the war, that Catherine began to indulge her great interest in gardens and landscaping. By this time she had come to favour the more informal style of English garden that was currently in vogue in Britain, rather than the rigid formality of French design. She also went to considerable lengths to get the best. One of her architects involved in garden design at Tsarkoye Selo, Vasilii Neyelov, was even dispatched to Britain. His mission was not just to study English garden design at first hand, but also to make contact with the appropriately named John Bush. Bush, who had been born Johann Busch in Hanover, had moved to London where he had started to earn a growing reputation with a successful nursery business in Hackney. Thanks to the intervention of Vasily Neyelov, Bush was persuaded to sell up and move his family to Russia to work for Catherine on a generous salary. For many years Bush was the Empress' principal gardener and was succeeded by his son Joseph in 1795.

As well as having favourite palaces, Catherine also had favourite cities in Russia. St Petersburg had made a good impression when she had arrived there many years ago in early 1744 *en route* to the court of Elizabeth. Though it was very much still a 'work in progress', the outlines of a great and well laid-out city were emerging. In contrast Catherine had disliked Moscow, the old capital, from the first time she had visited it. This was partly because the normally healthy Catherine had fallen ill soon after her arrival in 1744 and she thereafter associated the place with illness and misery. However the Empress also disliked the density of the city, describing it as *populous to the point of tedium*. Meanwhile in a letter from Moscow to an old family friend from Hamburg, Frau Bielcke, she wrote: *I prefer Petersburg, which is improving from day to day and in which I make everything work; whereas this city always seems to me to have the false look of Ispahan, which it loses, however, if I become angry.* Catherine's mention of Ispahan is a reference to Montesquieu's *Persian Letters*. Unlike the new St Petersburg, Moscow had a long history and its development had been influenced by Asia – especially the Mongols – and it had grown in a piecemeal, chaotic way. Psychologically one could say that St Petersburg represented the new Russia that Catherine wanted to mould in her own enlightened image, whereas Moscow represented the old, backward and chaotic Russia that the Empress was trying to change.[43]

St Petersburg was founded by Peter the Great on marshland in the Gulf of Finland in 1703 as his new capital, at the gateway of access to the Baltic Sea. It was built by soldiers and peasants working in awful conditions but people were soon attracted to the city, and it quickly grew to a population of more than 74,000 by 1750; by 1825 the figure was over 430,000. However when Catherine first saw it in 1744 many of the buildings were still log cabins and wolves and bears roamed the streets. Moscow was founded in the 12th century and by the 14th century had become the seat of the Russian Orthodox Church. It was in the rule of Ivan III, the Great (1440–1510), who freed the Russians from Tartar rule, that Moscow became a dominant political force at the heart of the Duchy of Muscovy and eventually Russia itself.

The onset of winter in 1770 put an end to that year's military campaigns, and though the end of the war was nowhere in sight, Catherine was generally in an upbeat mood. That winter she played host to an old acquaintance of hers, Prince Henry of Prussia, the brother of Frederick the Great. He had been touted as a possible future husband for her when she was a child. The main political purpose of Prince Henry's visit was to put forward the idea of a partition of Poland – in effect a partial carving-up of their mutual neighbour. Though Panin was against such an idea, it was gaining favour with Catherine and her officials. One of these was her old admirer Zakhar Chernyshev who, commenting on the aspirations of Poland's covetous neighbours, remarked: 'It is necessary, after all, that everyone have something.' It was a deeply cynical approach that Catherine seemed to share. The acquisition of Polish land was seen as an effective way of helping to pay for the costly war with the Turks. However, much of Prince Henry's visit seems to have consisted of an endless round of entertainment in both Moscow and St Petersburg. Catherine later wrote to Voltaire that: *From October to February there has been nothing but banquets, dances and spectacles. I do not know whether it is the effect on me of the last campaign, or whether joy is really universal in Russia.* Initially Catherine seems to have been concerned that the important guest would not enjoy himself. Yet she later wrote that she and the Prince had got on famously during his stay. *I have never in my life met anyone in whom I have found a greater conformity of ideas with my own than I find in him,* she wrote to Frau Bielke … *his disposition is cheerful and his character honest and humane, his mind elevated and polished; in a word he is a hero who shows me a great deal of friendship.*[44]

Though guests would come and go – and indeed so would wars – a recurring issue facing Catherine throughout her reign was the question of her son Paul. When Catherine was new to the throne and Paul was a child, his presence at the court had been useful for the Empress; he was a symbol of dynastic continuity masking her own lack of claim to the throne. Yet by late 1770 Paul was 16 and approaching the age of majority, a time when he might hope to become involved in some limited way in government. Ultimately this could even make him a rival for her position. The Empress, however, was in no mood for sharing power with her son, and never would be. Therefore though Paul's well-being was still crucial for Catherine, his main political 'role' for her was to maintain the family line, by getting married and having children. Thus like Elizabeth before her, by the late 1760s Catherine was busily scouring Europe for a suitable bride.

The Empress was keen to learn from her own experiences. Remembering the problems she had had as a young bride with an inexperienced husband, Catherine made sure that at the age of

14 her son Paul was given a practical sexual education. His tutor for this was a young widow whose father was a former provincial governor. The tutoring proved so successful that Paul became very close to her and in 1772 she had a son by him, though of course there was no question of legitimising the child, nor that Paul's infatuation with the woman – whose name was Sophia – could ever go any further. Meanwhile Paul's mother had begun the lengthy search for the right bride, and one which would not be completed for another couple of years. Although in theory Catherine had the pick of Europe, in practice her choices were more restricted. The idea of a Catholic bride entering the Russian imperial family would offend Orthodox nationalist sentiment – even though the bride would have to convert to Orthodoxy as Catherine had. This effectively ruled out Spain, France and of course Poland. In the end Catherine confined her search to a young German and Protestant princess, preferably from a family with no strong and thus complicating ties to either Austria or Prussia. This meant that she would choose someone of a very similar background to her own. However, she was also keen that as well as being politically and physically suitable, Paul's bride should be pleasing to him personally; given her own unhappy experience it is little wonder that she hoped for Paul and his bride to love each other.

As the methodical matchmaking process ground on, Catherine was busy too in defending her adopted country's honour – and that of her own. In 1768 a French cleric and astronomer, the abbé Chappe d'Auteroche, had published a book about his journey to Siberia back in 1761. At the time he had been welcomed by the Russians but now repaid their hospitality with a scathing attack on the country's backwardness, the laziness of its people, and also the Empress herself. The infuriated Empress could not let such an assault on Russia and her person go unchallenged. In 1770 a book called *The Antidote* was published and this was a lengthy and detailed rejection of the Frenchman's attacks on Russia. The author angrily declared that that was no other nation about which there had been uttered so many *untruths, absurdities and impertinences* as Russia. The author also condemned the Frenchman's *odious* suggestion that the ruler of Russia was a despot. The authorship of this long and somewhat tedious work was much speculated over; what few knew at the time was that it was written by Catherine herself. Though it was badly received by critics – including by Diderot – the fact that she felt compelled to write it was a sign of how jealously Catherine guarded both her and her adopted country's reputation.[45]

Russia's military prowess was also beginning to attract the attention – and concern – of the European powers as under the command of Prince Vasilii Dolgorukii her troops overran the Crimea peninsula in the summer of 1771. Catherine's aim was to install a pliable ruler as Khan of the Crimea, effectively putting it under Russian influence and removing it from the grasp of the Turks. Catherine was tantalisingly close to realising her aim of winning Russian access to the Black Sea. However, even as Russian troops advanced, another unseen but deadly menace was moving in the opposition direction, one that would trigger the start of a dangerous time for the Empress.

Plague and Potemkin 1771–3

From the beginning of the Russian war with the Turks there had been outbreaks of the disease that had once ravaged Europe and was still an intermittent threat in its southern reaches – bubonic plague.

Though she was aware of reports of the illness in the south, and had even hired a Greek medical expert to examine health precautions being taken around St Petersburg, Catherine does not appear to have been too concerned about the threat of plague in late 1769 and early 1770. In typically bold terms she wrote to Voltaire attacking foreign news reports that the disease was decimating the Russian army. *In the spring, evidently, those who have died of the plague will rise to fight again. The truth is that none of our troops has had the plague.*[46]

Nonetheless the disease began to make steady progress across parts of the Russian empire throughout 1770, including a serious if under-reported outbreak in Kiev. And by the time that Prince Henry of Prussia had paid a visit to the old capital Moscow in late 1770 there had already been an outbreak there, though both the Prince and the authorities seem to have been oblivious to it at the time. When the usual winter cold gripped that city and much of the rest of Russia by January 1771, it seemed as though any danger of a serious epidemic had passed. Then in March a more serious outbreak of plague based around a textile factory in Moscow made Catherine and the authorities realise that the threat was still very real. Once again prompt quarantine measures and a return of cold weather appeared to control the disease and there was renewed optimism that the outbreak was not serious. As late as May Catherine was even denying in her correspondence that Moscow had been hit by plague, suggesting that the illnesses there had simply been various different forms of fever. The Empress had meanwhile sponsored some secret experiments with possible plague treatment, which included the use of cold water, vinegar, ice and massage. She doubtless hoped to find the same effective way of dealing with the plague as she had found with smallpox.

From the start of summer Catherine began to receive yet more reports of plague in Moscow from her specially appointed administrator there, Senator Peter Eropkin. Strict controls on quarantine and the movement of people in and out of the city were imposed. Soon, however, the outbreak exploded into the streets. By late August around 400 people a day were dying from plague and the situation was becoming desperate. The city was soon in the grip of panic as well as plague. While its populace was

Bubonic plague was long associated by Russians with the lands ruled by the Ottoman Empire but there had not been a serious outbreak of the 'pestilential disorder', as it was known at the time, in Russia itself since the 1740s. This meant that most people concerned with public health in the country had not encountered the disease. In any case there had been no real medical advances in terms of understanding this deadly illness, and the link between the disease and the fleas and the rats who carry them was still not known. It was thought to be carried by people but also by clothes and be present in invisible vapours that might seep up from the ground. The standard control of the time was isolation and quarantine.

trapped inside by quarantine rules, many of the city's nobility had fled Moscow and even its governor General P S Saltykov wrote to Catherine in the second week of September begging to be allowed to leave the city. Two days later he left anyway, without waiting for a reply. By now up to 900 people a day were dying and the population, with most of the city's authorities having left, was in a mutinous mood. As violence broke out, the Archbishop Amvrosy – a man whom Catherine respected – tried to bring some calm to the city. Groups of city dwellers and peasants had begun to gather in crowds at a spot where a religious icon had been hung and which was believed to be working miracles. A chest was opened up to collect money to pay for a silver cover for the icon – though this may simply have been a money-making scam by unscrupulous people exploiting the situation. Suspecting that there was indeed corruption involved, and worried about the effect of the growing crowds, the Archbishop ordered that the chest be closed. However, the excited, suspicious and desperate populace feared that the Archbishop was trying to remove their beloved icon. In the violence that ensued a mob stormed the monastery where the Archbishop had taken shelter, dragged him outside and slaughtered him.

The savagery of events in Moscow both shocked and angered Catherine. On a personal level she was profoundly upset because she had appointed the Archbishop to his post and had approved of the way he had tried to tackle problems among the city's clerical administration. On a wider level the tragic events underlined her dislike and mistrust of Moscow; the Asiatic, uncontrolled and superstitious side of Russia. She wrote to Voltaire attributing the death of the Archbishop and the related Plague Riots to the fanatical nature of the city's population. *The famous Eighteenth Century really has something to boast of here! See how far we have progressed*, she wrote bitterly.[47]

The Empress' political response to the turmoil was to dispatch her favourite Grigory Orlov to Moscow, accompanied by troops and doctors, with orders to get a grip on the situation. Orlov had put himself forward for the mission and was a good choice for two reasons. After the ignominious flight of Saltykov, Catherine needed someone in charge in Moscow whom she could trust and who would carry the full authority of the crown. In addition her favourite had recently shown that he had a good head in a crisis when he had been called upon to deal with fires among the many wooden buildings of St Petersburg. Orlov and his entourage were quickly able to restore some order to the old capital, even if the plague itself took rather longer to bring under control. He reopened the public baths – whose closure had been a major source of discontent – promised freedom for serfs who worked in the hospitals, distributed food and clothing, burnt down 3,000 old and filthy buildings, disinfected many more and opened orphanages. Overall the soldier-turned-courtier impressed with his efficiency and also with the humanity with which he carried out his measures. The number of plague victims was still running at 600 or more a day in October, though thanks to Orlov's measures and especially a cold spell the numbers dwindled in November and December. However, it would not be for another year that all concern about the plague was removed. In all as many as 100,000 may have died in and around Moscow from the plague.

Catherine had been unnerved by the events in Moscow. She wrote, again to Voltaire, complaining that *Moscow is in a world of its own, not just a city.*[48] It was as if the disease and the violence it engendered were living, mocking symbols of Russia's past backwardness. In fact the plague eventually brought about some long needed public health measures in the old capital, including the demolition of many old houses and the placing of slaughterhouses and cemeteries outside the confines of the city.

The end of the Moscow plague crisis by the start of 1772 meant that Catherine could concentrate more fully on two pressing foreign issues facing her government – the fate of Poland and the continuing war with the Turks. By early 1772 Catherine was able to reach an agreement with Prussia and then Austria about what became known as the First Partition of Poland. In a formal convention signed in August 1772 Poland was to hand over to the three powers roughly one-third of her existing lands and population. This was eventually agreed to by a hapless and helpless Poland a year later. Meanwhile, Catherine had decided that the time was right to start peace talks with the Ottoman Empire and end the costly, lengthy war. A truce was reached in May 1772, pending the peace talks.

As far as Catherine was concerned the perfect man to head up the talks with the Turks in the summer of 1772 was Grigory Orlov. He had returned to St Petersburg from Moscow early in December 1771 to a hero's welcome for his efforts in dealing with that city's plague and public disorder. Orlov was also someone Catherine could rely on in such important talks, perhaps as a counterbalance to the influence of Nikita Panin, the chief official concerned with foreign affairs. One of the other main negotiators was to be Alexei Obreskov, the Russian envoy to the Ottoman Empire who had been freed from the Seven Towers in 1771. He had vast experience in dealing with the Turks – but he was also close to Panin. As with her appointment of Alexei Orlov as head of the naval expedition, Catherine was happy to overlook the fact that Grigory Orlov had virtually no experience in such complex and tricky negotiations. It seemed that Orlov, who had been at Catherine's side for a decade, had reached the zenith of his influence with the Empress.

If Catherine's foreign policy appeared to be moving relatively smoothly in the first half of 1772, there were nonetheless some alarms nearer to home. Once again they indirectly involved Paul. Back in 1771 there had been a curious episode involving a small band of exiled officers and minor nobles languishing in the outpost of Kamchatka, far away on Russia's remote Pacific coastline. They had staged a rebellion and fled, and later embarked on a series of meandering and historically unimportant adventures. What had caught Catherine's attention and unnerved her when she heard of the revolt was that the main had proclaimed allegiance to 'Emperor Paul Petrovich' – her son.

Much more worrying and closer to home was a plot uncovered in the spring of 1772 among some youthful officers and soldiers of the influential Preobrazhenskii Regiment. Their aim had apparently been to capture the Empress, and then take Paul from Tsarskoye Selo and name him emperor. Catherine would be sent to a monastery or handed over to her son for him to decide her fate. Once again the plotters invoked the name of Paul, even though the young Grand Duke had no inkling of their plans. The realisation that conspirators were willing to justify their actions in Paul's name was a constant pressure on the relationship between Catherine and her son. These conspirators escaped with their lives but were given severe corporal punishment and permanently exiled.

One of the grievances given by the young soldiers as justification for the plot was the growing power of Grigory Orlov. They had even claimed – and though such ideas were absurd they showed the kind of fevered gossip that could easily circulate – that Orlov was on his way south to the peace talks to secure the support of the army to become the Prince of Moldavia and even Emperor. Certainly Orlov seemed to be in a near-untouchable position. His recent heroics in dealing first with the fires in St Petersburg then with the plague in Moscow seemed to have cemented his already strong position in Catherine's life and her future. And yet, in the summer of 1772, Orlov's apparently unassailable position at court abruptly and dramatically changed.

The signal of Orlov's fall from grace came in two seemingly trivial court appointments. Early in August Catherine appointed a young Horse Guards officer Alexander Vassilchikov as a gentleman of the bedchamber. A month later the same 28-year-old was named adjutant-general and given an apartment in the Winter palace. It was now clear to the outside world – and Orlov himself – what some observant courtiers had suspected for some time. Catherine had chosen a new lover and favourite.

Orlov's reaction to the news of his replacement was dramatic. He abruptly left the peace talks with the Turks, which had anyway stalled over Russian demands about the status of the Crimea, and headed straight back for St Petersburg. However, Catherine barred his way and he was forbidden to enter the capital – on the pretext he had just came from a plague-ridden region – and he went instead to his estate at Gatchina, south of Tsarskoye Selo. From here Orlov began extended negotiations with Catherine over his future and his 'pay off' for being removed as favourite.

The precise reasons why Orlov fell from favour so swiftly are unclear. Catherine herself would later write that as he left for the peace talks, the Empress had learnt that Orlov had been serially unfaithful, most recent with a teenaged cousin of his. Orlov would have *remained for ever, had he not been the first to tire*, she claimed. Indeed it was said of him by an admittedly hostile commentator that when it came to women and sex 'Anything is good enough for him ... he loves like he eats'. Catherine's recollection, however, does not square with the content of the letters she wrote to friends after saying farewell to Orlov. In one she described him fondly as *without exaggeration the most handsome man of his time.*[49] These were hardly the words of a woman who felt scorned and betrayed. More likely perhaps is that there was a combination of factors. Catherine, who was 43, may have begun to feel intellectually bored with the man with whom she had shared so much, and have felt the desire for change. It is also possible that she may already have spotted Vassilchikov's charms when someone reminded her of the extent of Orlov's unfaithfulness – she must already have known of at least some of them – and that this helped make up her mind to act. Possibly Panin himself or one of his supporters helped ensure Catherine was kept aware of her favourite's faithlessness; the Panin faction were bitter rivals with the Orlovs and would have been keen to prise Grigory Orlov away from the Empress.

In any case, Orlov's fall from grace was not the complete break with Catherine that factions jealous of his family's influence may have wanted. Catherine was rarely, if ever, a vindictive person and she better than anyone knew the role he had played in putting her on the throne and the support he had since given her, emotionally and practically. Above all he was someone who had never sought to flatter or be obsequious, and she appreciated his frankness. Catherine was also keen not to alienate the Orlov clan as a whole and this can be seen in her generosity not just to Grigory but to his more potentially more dangerous brother Alexei too. As Catherine negotiated with her former favour at a distance, he and Alexei were awarded 10,000 serfs (i.e. the land on which 10,000 serfs worked). Grigory also received a generous annual pension of 150,000 roubles plus a lump sum to help set up a household in the Marble Palace across from the Winter Palace, and two silver services. He was also allowed to call himself Prince of the Holy Roman Empire, a title he had already been given but until now he had not been permitted to use. Meanwhile Catherine made it clear there were to be no awkward recriminations between them. Moreover, though Catherine and Grigory negotiated an agreement that to avoid embarrassment he should absent himself from the court for a year, this never happened. Indeed by May 1773, having already made one brief appearance at court, he returned to St Petersburg and resumed all his old offices – except that of official favourite.

The shifting status of Orlov from late 1772 into the middle of 1773 probably reflects both a period of uncertainty in the balance of power in the court and of a certain uncertainty in Catherine's personal life. It may be that she had regretted getting rid of Orlov as her lover so quickly. His replacement Vassilchikov was a pleasant-looking young officer with good manners, but had neither the physical charms nor the wit and intellect to excite Catherine. In choosing Vassilchikov she had probably deliberately gone for a very different character from the large, handsome bluff Orlov and had found the change unexciting. Yet emotionally she was probably unable to backtrack and rekindle her close relations with Orlov. At the same time, having Orlov and his brothers around was of great political comfort to Catherine as she faced growing political problems both at home and abroad.

Abroad, Catherine's main concern as 1773 wore on was that there still seemed no end to the costly war with the Turks. She was particularly dismayed that after a reluctant Rumiantsev had finally taken his troops across the Danube to attack the Turks in June, he had promptly withdrawn them again only a month later. The demands for fresh troops for the war also meant that once again Catherine had to authorise a levy of men in August 1773, the sixth since 1767. In all more than 300,000 had been called up since the start of the war and such levies inevitably caused tensions and unhappiness in the rural areas from which the men were drawn.

At home Catherine was again preoccupied over what to do with Paul. Her son had turned 18 in September 1772 and shown fresh signs of wanting to get involved in government. Catherine, however, was only interested in getting him married to a suitable bride who would quickly produce sons. By June 1773 she had narrowed her choice down to three German, Protestant sisters, the daughters of the Landgravin of Hesse-Darmstadt; they were duly invited to St Petersburg to be inspected by her and by her son. (A Landgrave, feminine Landgravine, was the ruler of a landgravate or territory.) Paul immediately fell for the middle of the three daughters, Princess Wilhelmina, who was 17 (the other two were 18 and 15) and Catherine too approved of the selection. Once she had made sure that Paul really was happy with his choice, Catherine suggested to the Landgravine that Wilhelma should marry him and become Grand Duchess. The Landgravine agreed and neither she nor her daughter opposed her compulsory conversion to Orthodoxy. Catherine wrote at the time how pleased she was with the way events had turned out. *{T}he middle one is everything we could ask for; she has a charming face, regular features, she is very affectionate and intelligent; I am very pleased and my son is smitten.*[50] Wilhelma converted to the Russian Orthodox faith in August and took the name Natalya, and the next day she and Paul were betrothed, just as Catherine and Peter had done many years before. They were married in St Petersburg that September.

Catherine's rather grim recollections of her own life as a grand duchess – plus her memory of own meddling in affairs of court at the time – prompted the Empress to draw up a series of maxims for her new daughter-in-law. The Grand Duchess was urged to learn Russian at once, to stay out of debt and of politics (unlike Catherine at that age) and to conform *herself to the tastes and habits* of her future husband – again, something that the young Catherine tried but conspicuously failed to do. Paul's future wife was also warned about getting involved with the *insinuations* of foreign diplomats at court. Some of this advice may seem hypocritical given Catherine's own past, but in fairness she was passing on the benefit of her own experiences and mistakes – as well as naturally making sure the Grand Duke and his wife did not try to establish an alternative power base.[51]

Apart from these helpful maxims, Catherine had also found ways to try to clip the wings of her son. Though she had allowed him to read some government reports, and had permitted him to take formal authority over his heredity lands of Holstein, Catherine had then arranged for Holstein to be ceded to Denmark. Moreover she did not set up a distinct new court for the newlyweds (as she and Peter had enjoyed) and she also made sure that now Paul was officially an adult, his governor Panin had to quit his rooms in the Winter Palace.

As 1773 drew to a close, the Empress was keener than ever to reach peace with the Turks, though at the same time she authorised plans for a new offensive from Rumiantsev across the Danube in the spring. In her personal life too, Catherine felt the need for fresh developments. Bored with her pleasant but rather dull new favourite, and unwilling to go back to Orlov, the Empress had someone else in mind. He was another officer, someone she had first noticed back in 1762 on the morning when she had ridden off at the head of her troops to ensure the abdication of her husband. Since then she had kept a close eye on his progress, promoted him, and kept in touch. Now it was time for Catherine to take the next step and bring him more permanently into her life. His name was Lieutenant-General Grigory Potemkin.

Catherine wrote a letter to Potemkin in early December 1773 while the latter was away at the front fighting under Rumiantsev. It is an odd, curiously restrained letter. In it Catherine writes ... *since on my part I am most anxious to preserve fervent, brave, clever and talented individuals I beg you to keep out of danger. When you read this letter, you may well ask yourself why I have written it. To this I reply: I've written this letter so that you should have the confirmation of my way of thinking about you, because I have always been your most benevolent, Catherine.*[52] The result of this letter was that as soon as his army had gone into their winter quarters – he had been in the thick of the action till then – Potemkin made his way as fast as possible to St Petersburg. He clearly saw this as a summons from Catherine. Indeed the letter really only makes sense in the

Grigory Alexandrovich Potemkin (1739–91) was born into a family of modest landowners not far from the city of Smolensk. A youth of considerable intelligence, and a gifted linguist, he studied Greek and ecclesiastical history at Moscow University but like many ambitious young men of his time joined the Guards and was stationed in St Petersburg. He was tall, well-built and good looking, though his looks were marred when he lost an eye in a riding accident. Through his relationship with Catherine he became one of the most powerful men in Russia, and was a statesman, administrator, soldier, lover of books and ideas, and was passionate about religion and Russia's many different peoples, especially his beloved Cossacks.

The intellect and vision of Grigory Potemkin made him the most important man to enter Catherine the Great's life

context of an existing correspondence and friendship between the pair. This is clear from Catherine's reference to giving *confirmation* of her way of thinking of him.

However, when he reached St Petersburg Catherine did not give Potemkin quite the welcome he had been expecting. Vassilchikov was still the favourite and the Empress showed little sign of changing that situation, even though she regularly met Potemkin whose brilliant company she evidently enjoyed. After some weeks of waiting around the court for a sign from the Empress, the impulsive Potemkin decided to force her hand. The officer, who had always been fascinated by religion, announced that he was to lead a monastic life and moved into a monastery, grew a beard, and prepared to take holy orders. Catherine, as Potemkin suspected she would, capitulated and sent her confidante Countess Bruce to fetch him. Very soon, some time at the start of February, they became lovers and so started the most important relationship of Catherine's life.

Though their very passionate physical relationship only lasted a relatively short time, Potemkin and Catherine remained bound together by the closest emotional and intellectual ties until his death just a few years before her own. He combined physical excitement and danger with great intelligence, passion, a wide-ranging lists of interest that included religion and other cultures, and had a fine political as well as military mind. His was to be a powerful influence on her and Russia's destiny over the next two decades. Now, however, theirs was essentially a love story as Catherine and Potemkin fell hopelessly in love with each other in the first half of 1774. Potemkin was just the man Catherine had been looking for to please her not just physically but emotionally too, and was someone with whom she could almost begin to share the burdens of rule. And as 1774 continued those burdens were increasing. Indeed, though she may have found the man of her dreams, Catherine was about to face the gravest threat of her reign.

Plots, Revolts and the Arts 1773–9

The early months of 1774 were an emotionally intense time for Catherine as her new relationship dominated her private life. The harmless but unfortunate Vassilchikov was moved out of his rooms in the Winter Palace and given a generous pay-off, while new rooms were decorated for Potemkin; his pride apparently prevented him from moving into the former apartment of another man. Meanwhile Potemkin wrote to Catherine asking to be made be an adjutant general to the Empress, a traditional title for a favourite. Catherine readily agreed and arranged it quickly, apparently delighted at his boldness. *I must confess that I am pleased that you, trusting me, decided to send your request directly to me without looking for roundabout ways*, she wrote to him.[53]

This letter from Catherine was one of many that the two lovers exchanged at this time, a feverish and passionate correspondence that could involve several letters a day, and delivered by courtiers even when they were within the same building. This correspondence was the eloquent 18th-century equivalent of an office romance today that might be conducted by e-mail, instant message or text. Though the conscientious Catherine did not neglect her official duties, the letters reveal just how much she had fallen for this extraordinary, vibrant character, whose earthy, almost animal qualities are reflected in her choice of pet names for him. To Catherine Potemkin was her *lion of the jungle, golden tiger, wolf, golden pheasant, dearest dove, part-bird part-wolf, little dog* and *kitten*. (Though to the Orlovs and others at court he was referred to as 'Cyclops' because he only had one eye.) On other occasions Catherine would allude to his love for 'exotic' peoples and call him her *Cossack* or *Tartar* or *Giaour*, the pejorative Turkish word for a non-Muslim. In one letter she freely confesses to the emotional hold that Potemkin has over her. *Oh Monsieur Potemkin! What a trick have you played to unbalance a mind, previously thought to be one of the best in Europe. It is time, high time, for me to become reasonable. What a shame! What a sin! Catherine II to be the victim of this crazy passion ... one more proof of your crazy power over me ... Well, mad letter, go to that happy place where my hero dwells.* Though the great patriot and loyal subject Potemkin usually addressed Catherine simply as 'Little Mother' (*Matushka*) or 'Sovereign Lady', his own letters were no less passionate. The one was equally in love with the other. One important difference, though, was that Potemkin was far more jealous than Catherine and became convinced that she had already had 15 lovers before him. She felt obliged to deny this in a *Sincere Confession* she wrote to him in February 1774. In it her list of lovers matches those already known about.[54]

The likely impact of Potemkin's rapid rise was not lost on observers at court, who quickly saw a new star emerging. The British representative in St Petersburg at the time, Sir Robert Gunning, may not have had a very high regard for Potemkin's looks, sullied as they were by the loss of his eye. 'His figure is gigantic and disproportioned, and his countenance is far from engaging,' he wrote. However, the diplomat praised the newcomer for having a 'great knowledge of mankind' and for possessing 'more of the discriminating faculty' than the Briton felt that Russians generally had. Sir Robert then wrote: 'A new scene has just opened here, which, in my opinion, is likely to merit more attention than any that has presented itself since the beginning of this reign.' The diplomat had seen at once that Potemkin was far more able than either of his two predecessors and that his emergence would change the balance of power at court.[55]

Though Catherine would remember 1774 fondly as the year in which she found the kind of thrilling love she had never felt before, it would also contain much darker memories. Up till now most of the threats to her rule – some of which had been significant but none too menacing – had mostly involved disgruntled guardsmen. They usually cited the name of Paul to legitimise their opposition to Catherine. However, there was another common form of protest against imperial rule in 17th- and 18th-century Russia, and this was the phenomenon of the so-called pretenders. These were people who claimed to be the true emperor and who sought to overthrow the current 'usurper'. During Catherine's reign alone there were more than 20 cases of people pretending to be either Ivan VI or Peter III, her late husband. The fact that both emperors were dead did not matter. It was part of the appeal of such pretenders that their 'true' fate had been suppressed, that they had really escaped, and had now returned to claim what was rightfully theirs. Nor did it matter that these pretenders, who were usually outsiders, misfits and often illiterate peasants, bore no resemblance to the monarch they were claiming to be. In Russia's vast remote lands and with its poor communications, very few people ever actually saw their

The Cossacks have played an important role in the history of Russia, notably as irregular cavalry fighting on the borders of Russia – not always for the same side – and what is now the Ukraine. Over the centuries the Cossacks were made up of runaway peasants and serfs, refugees from Poland and Turkey, and had developed a reputation as fierce fighters on horseback who lived on the margins of society and had their own rules and customs. There were different groups of Cossacks with their own names – including the Don Cossacks, the Yaik (later renamed the Ural Cossacks) Cossacks and the Zaporozhian Host from the Ukraine. Russian rulers, including Catherine, sought to bring them under more political and military control.

emperor. In the majority of cases, the activities of these pretenders came to very little. However by 1774 a pretender who claimed to be Peter III led an uprising that developed into what amounted to a peasant war and became the biggest threat that Catherine ever faced. The leader of this revolt was Emelyan Pugachev.

Pugachev was a Don Cossack, that is a Cossack from the area of the River Don. No one is sure when he was born, but it is known that Pugachev was an illiterate army deserter who had fought in the war against the Turks, had been travelling under the guise of an wealthy merchant and had made his way to join the Yaik Cossacks. By November 1772 he was claiming that he was Peter III. Pugachev/Peter explained his appearance now by suggesting that he had escaped death in 1762 and instead travelled abroad. Now he was back to protect the Cossacks' age-old rights. The name of Peter III had resonance among many of Russia's poor, especially among the serfs; it was widely if wrongly believed that the Emperor's proclamation freeing nobles from state service was to have been followed by a similar one freeing the serfs. Some felt that this measure had been thwarted by the coup organised by the German 'usurper' Catherine.

Pugachev's first attempt at impersonation came to nothing as he was soon arrested, and in the spring of 1773 Catherine was signing the order for him to be flogged and exiled to Siberia. Yet the resourceful and wily Cossack managed to escape and by September of 1773 had re-appeared amongst the Yaik. Now his claims to be Peter III started to be accepted by the disgruntled Cossacks. As part of his pretence, he showed people marks on his body which he claimed were the 'Tsar's marks', though in reality they were scars from an old illness. And while Pugachev could not read or write, he appears to have been a gifted demagogue well able to convince his audience of his right to rule as he cunningly told them exactly what they wanted to hear. Slowly people began to join his movement which grew in size and power in the autumn of 1773.

The Empress and her advisers initially misjudged the serious-ness of the affair and sent General Vasilii Kar off to quash it with an inadequate force. The General was soon beaten back by the rebellious Cossacks and he was humiliatingly forced to retreat to Moscow. Now Catherine dispatched a more powerful force under the command of the reliable General Alexander Bibikov, who knew the area well and who was also given wide powers to inves-tigate the cause of the rebellion. Many suspected that agents of foreign states were involved.

Catherine herself was somewhat distracted at the time by the arrival at court of the French thinker Denis Diderot, whose work she had long admired and whom she had patronized. He stayed for five months and the two enjoyed numerous long conversations. Later the philosopher described Catherine as being the 'soul of Caesar with all the seductions of Cleopatra ...' and of having the 'soul of Brutus in the body of Cleopatra'. At the time Catherine was flattered by Diderot and was very gracious towards him, if occasionally irked by his ignorance of Russia. Years later however she was to criticise his abstract approach to philosophy and gov-ernment, and she felt it increasingly hard to bridge the reality gap between philosopher and ruler – a sad conclusion for someone who aspired to be a philosopher empress. She also described his criticism of her 'Great Instruction' as a *piece of genuine twaddle*.[56] However, Diderot's visit did at least enable Catherine to get to know a man who would play a major role in the following two decades as one of her best friends and correspondents – Melchior Grimm, a close friend of Diderot.

Catherine's astute decision to send Bibikov to the Orenburg region where the rebels were based seemed to have paid off in the early spring of 1774 when the general defeated Pugchev's forces. Even though the unfortunate Bibikov fell ill and died before the operations to put down the unrest had been completed, it was widely assumed that this it was only a matter of time until this

The unlikely friendship between Catherine and the philosopher Denis Diderot withered afer his criticisms of Russian life were printed

happened; this meant Catherine and the court turned their full attentions back once more to the draining war with the Turks.

Pugachev, however, was not so easy to get rid of as the Empress had supposed – or indeed as the real Peter III had been. By summer Pugachev's rebellion had burst back into life and with up to 20,000 fighting men under him, the rebel leader sacked the city of Kazan in early July. It was a scene of carnage with noblemen murdered and women raped, killed or taken prisoner. This was of course a city that Catherine had admired when she had journeyed on the Volga many years before and this only made more personal the horror of what had now happened there. Meanwhile vast swathes of the countryside were in the grip of unrest, with rebellious serfs rising up to butcher their landowners. Catherine was facing what was in effect a peasant war. Pugachev himself had organised his headquarters in a kind of grotesque parody of the imperial court. His leading supporters even took the name of real officials – one called himself 'Count Panin'. Meanwhile 'court' secretaries wrote out the 'Emperor's' proclamations in several different languages to be

Friedrich Melchior Grimm (1723–1807) had come to St Petersburg in 1773 as part of the German entourage for the marriage of Natalya (formerly Wilhelma) to Grand Duke Paul. A nobleman and author, Grimm was already known to Catherine as an author of a kind of elite cultural newsletter to which she subscribed. Though he refused her offer of a position in her service they became friends and began a long and remarkable correspondence that lasted for the rest of the Empress' life; it covered all topics including even the behaviour of her beloved greyhounds. Grimm also helped select European art for Catherine to buy, and she helped him financially.

distributed in the region. However the astute leader Pugachev did make one mistake; he married his mistress, something that struck supporters as odd –'Peter III' was surely already married to the woman they were trying to overthrow, Catherine II.

Pugachev's success in taking poorly-defended Kazan was short-lived as his forces were soon defeated again by imperial troops. However, at the real imperial court there was a mounting sense of panic about Pugachev's revolt, with fears that he might take his motley troops and head towards Moscow, the old capital and still the true heart of Russia. Catherine reluctantly agreed to put Peter Panin in charge of the operation against Pugachev. He was a skilled and tough soldier but she distrusted him, and he made little secret of his antediluvian belief that only men were fit to rule Russia. It was a belated political victory for Peter Panin's brother Nikita, whose influence had been gradually waning. Significantly, though, he had sought to win over Potemkin to his position.

In the end, Peter Panin's role was not decisive in hastening the end of the unrest. Pugachev's defeats soon after taking Kazan had weakened him and during the next few weeks he and his troops rampaged savagely but aimlessly around the countryside until they were beaten again at Tsaritsyn at the end of August. Then the Cossacks, realising the rebellion was doomed, betrayed their own impostor emperor in an effort to save themselves. This time Pugachev did not escape and he was eventually brought to Moscow for interrogation. Catherine briefed the inquisitors by letter, and in particular wanted to know who had really been behind the rebellion – she could hardly believe this uneducated Cossack had been the prime mover. However Pugachev's answers gradually allayed Catherine's fears. She wrote to Voltaire – again, knowing that this would become widely known – that *So far there is no shred of evidence that he was the tool of any outside power or intelligence or under anyone's influence. It is to be supposed that Monsieur Pugachev is the master brigand, and not a servant.*[57]

Though she had been badly shaken by this bloody revolt, this did not stop Catherine from showing her customary humanity and dislike of gratuitous punishment. First she sent her trusted Procurator-General Viazemskii to Moscow to oversee the handling of the prosecution of Pugachev and the other ringleaders. In doing so she secretly urged him to keep the number of executions down to a minimum and to avoid any torture of the condemned during their execution. *Please help to inspire everyone with moderation both in the number and the punishment of the criminals ... We do not have*

The most threatening rebellion of Catherine's long reign was lead by Emelyan Pugachev

to be clever to deal with barbarians. The judges meanwhile urged that Pugachev be broken on the wheel — a truly hideous process

– arguing that his original sentence of being quartered and then beheaded was too lenient. Viazemskii persuaded them to stick to their first sentence. Then, knowing that the Empress would deplore the idea of a man being publicly cut into quarters while still alive, Viazemskii privately arranged for the executioner to make a 'mistake' and behead the miserable prisoner before quartering him. This was done, to the shock of the expectant crowd in Moscow's Bolotnaia Square in January 1775. Catherine's request for no torture and a minimal number of death sentences did not just reflect her own compassion; she also wanted to avoid staining the reputation both of Russia and its enlightened Empress.[58]

Though the Pugachev revolt had failed and neither Moscow nor Catherine's rule had been under immediate threat, the scale of it had shaken the Empress. In particular she had wobbled in giving military authority to a man she disliked and mistrusted – Peter Panin – at the height of the crisis. Yet this was the last comparable crisis that Catherine was to face in her reign, even if the flow of pretenders and exotic impostors was not finished. (They included a mysterious woman who styled herself Countess or Princess Elizabeth and who had been wandering around Europe apparently claiming to have been the daughter of the late Empress Elizabeth; she was tricked on board a Russian ship in the Mediterranean by Alexei Orlov, taken to Russia and imprisoned where she died of consumption in late 1775.) Moreover, at the height of the crisis Catherine had received news of something for which she had long waited – a successful peace treaty with the Ottoman Empire and an end to war.

The Treaty of Kuchuk-Kainardzhi – a village in what is now Bulgaria – was signed in July 1774 and was a triumph for Catherine, her powerful new advisor Potemkin and also Field Marshal Rumiantsev, who had forced the hand of the Turks in the negotiations. The terms delighted Catherine. Under the agreement, the khanate of Crimea was to be independent – free from Ottoman control though not Russian influence – and Russia gained the fortress ports of Kerch, Enikalke and Kinburn, the right for Russian merchant ships to pass through the Turkish straits in the Black Sea and an ill-defined but important agreement that was to mean Russia had a say over the lives of the Orthodox peoples living under Ottoman rule. The most important outcome was that Catherine had achieved what even Peter the Great had not managed – a strong Russian presence on the Black Sea and every prospect of gaining control over the coveted Crimean peninsula. Little wonder that Catherine dispensed praise, titles, lands and money in the direction of Rumiantsev, as well as other senior military staff. She also organised lavish celebrations in the summer of 1775 in Moscow – her first visit there for some years – to mark the first anniversary of the signing of the treaty. These featured fireworks, parades and even mock-ups of the Black Sea and Russia's new territory there. Catherine was fulfilling her own and Russia's long-cherished destiny and wanted the world to know it.

Potemkin, meanwhile, had been firmly established in his position as favourite, acquiring far more power and influence than Grigory Orlov had ever obtained. He had been made governor of Russia's new territories in the south that bordered the Crimea, vice-president of the College of War, and was put in charge of all of Russia's irregular forces – his favourites, the Cossacks. In doing this he eclipsed not just the Panin faction but also the Orlovs and the Chernyshev faction. The undermined Zakhar Chernyshev eventually resigned as Minister of War while Orlov had an angry meeting with Catherine in June 1774 about Potemkin's rise to power. In 1775 he left on a two-year European tour while his brother Alexei left state service.

Potemkin was fast becoming not just a favourite, but a statesman too. It is also possible that he acquired yet another status – that of Catherine's husband. A persistent story suggests that Catherine secretly married her lover, possibly during a late-night ceremony in the Church of St Sampson in St Petersburg early in June 1774. However, no proof of the wedding has ever emerged, even if Catherine did refer to Potemkin as her *darling husband*.[59] We will probably never know for sure whether they married. In any case the pair would soon find how difficult it was to reconcile their evident love for each other with their strong personalities and official duties. Indeed, if Catherine was married to anyone or anything, it was above all to her role as Empress of All the Russias.

Catherine's eternal preoccupation with her duty as Empress was shown by her personal drafting of important local government reforms, usually known as the Guberniya Reform. This was her response to the administrative weaknesses of Russia that had been brutally exposed by both the plague riots and the Pugachev revolt. The empress spent months working on the legislation – in what she told Grimm was a new bout of *legislomania*. Unlike the previous efforts – the Legislative Commission and her 'Great Instruction' – which she said had involved *principles only*, this new spurt involved *earnest work*. In fact the Empress drew on both her own previous work and that of the Legislative Commission to produce this wide-ranging reform, which was made public in November 1775.[60] It reorganised Russia's provinces, decentralised local government and established a new network of courts, but also made provision for social welfare and education. This was a large-scale reform of the system and the aims of which – making Russian governance more effective, modern and just – were close to Catherine's heart. Catherine hoped and believed that new structures could help change the way Russia was governed.

Two people who helped Catherine form this legislation were Potemkin and a 37-year-old Ukrainian officer by the name of Colonel Peter Zavadovsky, a protégé of Rumiantsev. The three of them spent a considerable amount of time working and dining together. Then in early January 1776 the well-educated, slightly reserved Zavadovsky was named adjutant-general to the Empress – the traditional title given to the new favourite.

At first glance this looks like a rapid fall from favour by Potemkin. In fact Potemkin kept all his offices and remained the dominant voice at court, second only to Catherine. What seems to have happened is that while Catherine and Potemkin still loved each other – and always would – they both found it hard to cope with this relationship and the inescapable fact that she was empress and he her subject. Potemkin was brilliant, intelligent, witty and daring – but he was also very insecure, jealous and sulky. This made their intense relationship a battleground, and neither of them coped well with the strain. Catherine once wrote that to him that *We would be happier if we loved each other less.* The promotion of Zavadovsky seems to have been an attempt by Catherine to find a new and less emotionally draining lover as a way out of this impasse, while retaining Potemkin as a close and powerful advisor. Potemkin seems to have fluctuated between acceptance of the new situation and anger at it, and on one occasion he demanded the new favourite's removal. But despite the feverish speculation and hopes of his enemies, his power at court remained largely undiminished.[61]

In April the court was thrown into fresh turmoil when the Grand Duchess Natalya died in childbirth, along with her child. This was of course a personal tragedy for Paul, who was utterly distraught at his loss. For Catherine, however, though she was genuinely moved by her daughter-in-law's death and her son's grief, this was also a blow to the throne. Catherine was anxious for Paul to produce an heir, someone who could rule after him – or, just possibly, instead of him if as she was slowly beginning to fear he was as unsuitable to govern as her late husband Peter had been. So while Prince Henry of Prussia – fortuitously visiting Russia – comforted Paul she immediately set about choosing a successor for Natalya and drew up a plan of action. Though this may appear

A contemporary silhouette of Catherine and her family in the palace gardens at Tsarskoye Selo

callous, it was more a sign of Catherine's very practical nature; the dynasty had to come first.

Catherine's choice was a girl whom she had always wanted him to marry, though she had been considered too young the first time round. This was Princess Sophia Dorothea of Württemberg, yet another German princess. According to the Empress she herself succeeded in coaxing a reluctant Paul to get over his grief and to accept a new bride. The fact that Catherine was able to inform her son that his late wife had been conducting an affair with a friend of his made this task less difficult. In any case mother and son seem genuinely to have been quite close during this period, something that had not always been the case and would not be in the future. Little time was now wasted. Paul travelled to Berlin with Prince Henry in July 1776 where he met and liked the intelligent and attractive 16-year-old Princess Sophia. By September they were both in Russia where Sophia converted to the Russian Orthodox church, taking the name Maria Fyodorovna, and the pair were betrothed the next day. By the end of the month the pair were married.

By early 1777, however, Catherine's relationship with Zavadovsky was not going well. The Ukrainian was by nature a born administrator, not a courtier, and certainly lacked Potemkin's mental robustness. He genuinely loved Catherine and his nerves suffered from the pressure of the relationship and the fact that it was conducted in the goldfish bowl of court life. The continuing presence of Potemkin cannot have made his life much easier either. For his part Potemkin had come to terms with his and Catherine's new relationship, which though no longer the physical romance of old was a deep, powerful and enduring friendship. Indeed it seems to have been Potemkin himself who introduced a bold and handsome young protégé to Catherine, a new face who was to become the first of a succession of young lovers who were to receive the Empress' affections.

Revolving Doors 1777–87

By 1777 Catherine was in her late forties and though she had lost none of her charm and poise, her looks had started to fade. She had put on weight and took to hiding her growing size with loose-fitting robes. Meanwhile her health, while generally still robust, was just starting to deteriorate. Nonetheless Catherine was intellectually as sharp as ever and the next decade would see further reforms as the ambitious Empress sought to continue her process of modernising Russia. On the foreign front, too, Catherine would soon be close to realising a dream that Russia had long held – obtaining full control over the Crimea and establishing herself as a major power in the Black Sea.

The Empress' private life, meanwhile, would be no less busy over the next decade; indeed at times it would seem almost chaotic. This was the period when the middle-aged Catherine took on a succession of handsome young favourites and the time when the office of court favourite became institutionalised. This was the time, too, from which her unfair reputation as a woman who was sexually insatiable dates. In fact there is no evidence that Catherine had an especially high sex drive. Instead, like many people, she had an emotional need to love and be loved.

In any case, the rapid turnover of favourites was usually due to their lack of suitability for the role – or in one case death – rather that a constant desire on Catherine's part for new partners. Yet though Catherine was usually perfectly able to separate her role as a woman from that of being ruler, this did not stop foreign diplomats and others criticising her personal affairs and gossiping over possible future candidates to be the new favourite, often in the most ribald terms. In 1778 the British envoy Sir James Harris graphically claimed that the Empress preferred a number of different loves as 'the Gratification of this disgraceful Passion is now become a Distemper rooted in the Blood'. Her excess of passion would lead to an early death, he – wrongly – predicted.[62]

The first in this new line of favourites was a handsome, brave 31-year-old officer of Serbian origin called Semyon Zorich, who had been a prisoner of war of the Turks for five years. Potemkin, who was to acquire a reputation as a provider of young officers who might take Catherine's fancy, introduced the officer to the Empress. The inveterate womaniser Potemkin and Catherine clearly had a relationship that was no longer threatened by the other having partners. A tearful Zavadovsky, meanwhile, who had never seemed quite able to cope with the emotional pressures of his role, was given a decent pay-off which included the now obligatory silver service. The Empress would make use of his administrative talents in her future education reforms.

For a while Catherine seemed delighted with Zorich's lively charms and was also happy when her original favourite, the ageing Grigory Orlov, had married his own first cousin. At the end of 1777 Catherine was even more delighted at news for which she had long waited – a grandson. Her new daughter-in-law Maria Fyodorovna had given birth to a healthy boy, who was called Alexander. From now on this first-born grandson would become a major part of Catherine's life and her plans for the future. Unable to look after her own son as she had wished, Catherine was determined that Alexander would be brought up in a more modern way; she hoped too that unlike his father the child could be turned into a model future emperor and she was to make detailed provision for his education. His birth was marked in 1778 by some very elaborate and exotic celebrations, masterminded by the inventive Potemkin.

By the spring of 1778 Catherine seemed to have tired of the uncultured and brazen Zorich, who had also made the mistake of quarrelling badly with Potemkin. So when Potemkin introduced another handsome young officer, Ivan Rimsky-Korsakov, Catherine quickly transferred her affections. By the beginning of July Zorich had been paid off and the 24-year-old Rimsky-Korsakov – who was a fine singer and had an excellent ear for music, as befits an ancestor of the composer Nikolai Rimsky-Korsakov – was firmly established as favourite. Catherine, who was always genuinely upset during such upheavals in her private life, was also hit hard by news that her regular correspondent and champion Voltaire had died. She wrote to Grimm that when she heard the news confirmed *all at once I had a reaction of universal discouragement and felt a very great contempt for all the things of this world.* As a last gesture to Voltaire she made plans to buy his entire library. Approaching 50, Catherine would increasingly find that many of the key figures in her life were starting to disappear.[63]

Amid all this emotional turmoil, Catherine continued her attempts to make Russia in general and St Petersburg in particular a cultural capital. Apart from acquiring Voltaire's books, the Empress made plans to have Raphael's famous loggias (walls and arches that had been painted under the artist's supervision) in the Vatican Palace copied in St Petersburg, and bought a collection of more than 200 paintings that had belonged to Sir Robert Walpole. This last purchase was widely seen as sign of Russia's growing cultural importance and power. In 1779 she also hired the Scottish architect Sir Charles Cameron, who built what became the Cameron Gallery at Tsarskoye Selo, plus the Italian architect Giacomo Quarenghi. She had even learnt to appreciate music, thanks to the works of the new court musician, the popular Italian composer Giovanni Paisiello, who stayed at court from

A print of Catherine and her beloved greyhounds in the park of the Peterhof Palace. The popularity of this breed of dog in Russia has endured across the centuries

1776 to 1784. In all Catherine lived a busy and varied life. She amused herself with books, her writing, art, gardens, architecture, her greyhounds — whom she took on early morning walks when possible – and of course her beloved grandson Alexander upon whom the Empress doted.[64]

In April 1779 Maria Fyodorovna once more justified the great hopes Catherine had always held for her when she gave birth to a second son. Significantly he was given the Greek name of Constantine. The birth of a second grandson all but assured the future succession. Catherine now had no need of any other potential successors. Accordingly she moved the brothers and sisters of the murdered Ivan VI from their discreet confinement in Russia to Denmark, where they were well looked-after – but also kept under close supervision lest they ever became potential figureheads for opposition.

By the autumn of 1779 Catherine's emotional life was once more in turmoil. Rimsky-Korsakov, the man she dubbed her *Pyrrhus, King of Epirus* because of his Greek-style *ancient beauty*, had been betraying her with another woman. To make matters worse the other woman was Catherine's old friend and confidante Countess Bruce, who had become infatuated with the

It was no accident that Catherine's second grandson was called Constantine, and he was even given a Greek nurse. Catherine's so-called Greek Project envisaged the dismembering of the Ottoman Empire in Europe and the founding of a new Greek empire ruled by Constantine from Istanbul – formerly called Constantinople and once capital of the old Orthodox Byzantine empire. A new state meanwhile would be set up in Moldavia-Wallachia, to be called by the old Roman name of Dacia. It was therefore deemed essential for Russia to have an agreement with Austria, whose lands bordered this area. The project – never ultimately realised – was enthusiastically supported by Potemkin but opposed by Panin, who realised it meant the end of the old Prussian alliance.

arrogant young officer. She had found the pair in a compromising position and had been one of the last to know or at least guess at their affair.[65] Indeed the officer then went on to break Countess Bruce's heart with an affair with the much younger and more beautiful Countess Ekaterina Stroganova, who was married to a Russian grandee. Catherine was distraught and angry, and Rimsky-Korsakov was sent off to Moscow. However, once again the discarded favourite was given generous gifts.

If Catherine's last two choice of favourites – each suggested by Potemkin – had been poor ones, her next one proved to be far better. In 1780 the Empress herself singled out the 23-year-old Horse Guards officer Alexander Lanskoy and it proved to be a happy match. Lanskoy, a nobleman of modest background, was handsome, unassuming, of a gentle nature and though not well educated or especially cultivated he was eager to learn. In effect their relationship seems to have been that of part lovers, part teacher and pupil and part mother and son – something which would not have been lost on the increasingly alienated Paul, her real son. There is little doubt that Lanskoy genuinely loved the Empress and she in turn seems to have loved him. Importantly, he knew his place, did not become involved in politics and accepted the omnipresence of Potemkin. In many ways he was the ideal companion for Catherine at this time in her life, and though there were unconfirmed rumours that she briefly dallied with another courtier in 1781, she was to stay contentedly with him for several years.

For some time Catherine – despite the more aggressive urging of advisers such as Potemkin and the up-and-coming Alexander Bezborodko – had been cautious in her conduct of foreign affairs, especially in relation to the south and the Turks. The last thing Russia needed was another costly war. This did not however stop her imposing her own candidate in the now supposedly independent Tartar Khanate of the Crimea. Then in 1780 she agreed to meet Emperor Joseph II at his request on New Russian territory at Mogilyov on the river Dnieper. It was the second time she had met a foreign ruler in recent years – her relative Gustavus II or 'cousin Gu' had come to Russia three years before. And like the Swedish king, Joseph was travelling incognito – his chosen name was Count

Falkenstein. The meeting was timed to coincide with Catherine's already announced plans to make a tour of the provinces to see how her 1775 reforms were bedding down.

Though it was hot and she was troubled by clouds of mosquitoes, Catherine's meeting with Joseph II on 24 May 1780 proved a great success. The two monarchs got on well and this proved the start of an important political relationship. Later Joseph came to visit her at Tsarskoye Selo. Catherine was clearly impressed with the young emperor, who at that time still ruled with his mother Maria Theresa. She wrote to Grimm: *If I were to begin singing his praises I would never finish; he has the soundest most profound, most learned brain that I know*. In letters to Catherine, the Austrian emperor was equally flattering about her, praising her 'energy, bravery and constancy'.[66] The practical outcome of their friendship came the following year when in May 1781 – some months after the death of Maria Theresa, no fan of Catherine's – Russian and Austria reached a secret agreement. In an exchange of letters between Joseph and Catherine the Austrians agreed to support Russia in the event of any dispute arising between the Russians and Turks from their 1774 treaty. Crucially the agreement – which comprehensively signalled the end of the influence of the pro-Prussian Panin faction – gave Catherine and her advisors more room for manoeuvre in their handling of the Crimea.

Catherine was worried that Russia's closer relations with Austria – at the expense of Prussia – might further harm her relationship with Paul. The young man, whose governor had been the Prussophile Panin, had inherited his father's love for all things military and Prussian. Catherine, with the aid of her new friend Joseph, thought that a voyage abroad and a warm welcome in imperial Vienna would help reconcile the Grand Duke and Grand Duchess to the new political climate; the idea was that Joseph himself would inform Paul of the alliance. Panin, however, tried to scare Paul and Maria into believing such a trip was a pretext for getting them out of the country and losing control of their sons (who were at that time being inoculated against smallpox under the care once again of Dr Dimsdale). For a time Paul, who was also annoyed at no provision being made for a trip to Berlin, effectively refused to go on the trip until the direct intervention of Catherine and Potemkin.

Though correspondence between Catherine and her son and daughter-in-law during their long trip seems friendly and genuine enough, another incident arose that once more reminded the Empress of the potential threat her son posed. In early 1782 court officials intercepted a letter from a young man called Pavel Bibikov – son of the general – to one Prince Alexander Kurakin, a nephew of Panin who was travelling with Paul. In this letter Bibikov deplored the situation in Russia under Catherine's reign, attacked the influence of Potemkin – the 'Cyclops par excellence' – as the root cause of many of the country's problems and said that the only hope for the future was the Grand Duke Paul.

A furious and alarmed Catherine immediately ordered an investigation and Bibikov was arrested and interrogated. No evidence of any real plot was found, but the Empress did write to her son – then in Italy – making clear her displeasure at Bibikov's *impudent acts*. In a later letter Catherine explained to Paul and his wife how in being lenient to Bibikov – he was exiled to Astrakhan – she had *pulled this young man ... back from the abyss*. She then added: *I tell you this, my dear children, because my tenderness for you wishes that you make use of this for the present time and that to come.* Despite the warm words, Catherine's meaning was not lost on Paul – he was to stay well clear of any plots and possible conspirators. When he returned to Russia a chastened Grand Duke – who while critical of his mother had never been involved in any conspiracy – wisely kept a low profile.[67]

Despite all the machinations at court, her complicated private life and her concern about the south and the Greek Project,

Catherine still carried out fresh reforms in Russia that aimed to build on the work of the Legislative Commission and the reforms of 1775. Thus in 1782 she introduced what is usually called the Police Code, though literally it was the Code of Good Order. This provided a detailed set of provisions for the maintenance of good order and morals in urban areas, and was very moral in tone. For example it condemned public gambling and drunkenness. In 1785 there followed a reform known as the Charter to the Towns which was a wide-ranging reform of urban government. It was accompanied by the Charter to the Nobility that confirmed and added to the established rights of the nobility. This last piece of legislation has been variously and widely interpreted; some see it as Catherine introducing the first concept of civil rights into Russia, while others see it as a capitulation by the Empress to the power of the nobility. In general, however, all her legislation was based in some part on enlightenment ideas gleaned from her readings, and drew largely on her Great Instruction and the work of the Legislative Commission.

Another key reform overseen by Catherine in the 1780s was in education, a subject that was always close to the Empress' heart. Whether aimed at her grandsons or at society as a whole, Catherine enthusiastically shared the Enlightenment view that education could be a powerful tool for good. In 1782 her former favourite Zavadoksky was put in charge of the new Commission on National Education, which was to oversee the training of teachers, the writing of new textbooks and the building of schools. Influenced by Austria and the Emperor Joseph – who sent her an advisor on educational policy – Catherine had decided that a system of schools had to be provided by the Russian state. In 1786 the Statute of National Schools aimed to set up a secondary school in each provincial capital and a primary school in each district town. By the end of the century the system would produce 315 schools, 90 teachers and teach around 20,000 pupils – a tenth of them girls. Though she was now in her fifties and had been in power for two decades, Catherine still wanted change in Russia – even if strictly on her own terms.[68]

The year 1783 was a bitter-sweet one for the Empress. All around her she seemed to be losing old friends and advisers. First a loyal officer General Bauer died, prompting a typical outburst against the medical profession. *I curse all doctors, surgeons and the whole faculty*, Catherine wrote to Grimm. *They have killed off another person who was close to me for thirty-three years.* Then in quick succession both Nikita Panin and Grigory Orlov, who had been deteriorating fast in recent years, died. Though the Empress had never completely trusted Panin he had been there from the start of her reign and his departure was a reminder of her own mortality. As for Orlov, he had been an immense support both before and after she became ruler,

The Crimea was a strategically important peninsula on the Black Sea that had long been fought over, right back to Ancient Greek times and before. Later it became for a while a Roman tributary state. In the 13th century it was occupied by the Mongols and in the 15th century was established as a khanate under Crimean Tartars and fell under the influence of the Ottoman Empire. Russia had long coveted it as a gateway to the Black Sea and in 1737 Russian forces had briefly entered the peninsula. Potemkin famously described the Crimea as the pimple on Russia's nose.

and Catherine felt his loss keenly. She wrote to Grimm: *Although I was very prepared for this sad event…I feel the most acute affliction over it; in him I lose a friend and the man to whom I have the greatest obligations in the world and who rendered me the most essential services.* She later described it as a *black year*.[69]

In contrast, Catherine's and Potemkin's plans to increase Russian power in the Black Sea at last came to fruition. In 1782 Catherine had unveiled the statue of Peter the Great by Falconet in St Petersburg, with the simple but powerful inscription: 'To Peter the First from Catherine the Second'. Now she would have a

A modern photograph of the statue of Peter the Great in St Petersburg, Catherine's inscription to him is visible

rather more tangible tribute to the great emperor's memory – the Crimea.

Potemkin, whose authority and power in Russia was second only to Catherine's, had been making preparations to seize the peninsula and in late 1782 the Empress gave him secret instructions to carry out the annexation if disputes with the Ottoman Empire continued. Though dogged by ill-health – the Empress too suffered bouts of fever – Potemkin initiated the plan in the spring of 1783. Catherine's impatience grew, however, as days turned into weeks and there was still no news of events in the Crimea. Her letters to her one-time lover and closest of friends reflected this feeling. Then, at last, in late July came the news Catherine had been waiting for – the people of the Crimea had taken an oath of allegiance to Russia. This crucial gateway to the Black Sea now belonged to Catherine and the Russian Empire. Once she had got over her irritation at not being kept regularly informed of events, Catherine was effusive in her praise to Potemkin. *For all the labours exerted by your and the boundless cares for my affairs I cannot sufficiently expound my recognition to you*, she wrote to him.[70] The achievement was even greater because it had happened without provoking another war with the Turks. The Crimea was incorporated formally into Russia in February 1784 and known as the Tauride Region; Potemkin became its governor-general.

The joy that Catherine felt at this great foreign policy achievement was however blighted by a personal tragedy. She had already been upset a year earlier when her beloved Lanskoy fell off a horse and was ill for six weeks. Now in June 1784 her favourite was taken seriously ill with an inflammation of the throat. Within days, he had died – probably from diphtheria, though there were all sorts of salacious rumours that he had taken too many aphrodisiacs. Catherine was utterly distraught. She was plunged into a deep depression, staying in her rooms for three weeks, and being unable to conceal her sorrow for months to come. For some time the Empress even refused to have the decomposing corpse of her favourite buried, as though unwilling to part with his last tangible remains. She later said that she hovered between *life and death* at this time. In Lanskoy, Catherine thought she had found the man who would be by her side for the rest of her life. Even the return of Potemkin – who was sent for by worried couriers – initially failed to console Catherine. It took all the statesman's care and the passing of time for Catherine to overcome the worst of her grief. However, even during the darkest days she did not neglect affairs of state. She told Grimm that *during the most frightful moments I was asked for orders for everything and I gave them well, with order and intelligence.*[71]

As Catherine overcame her grief she filled her already busy life with yet more activities. She and her circle of friends and courtiers began writing plays, including one called *Le Trompeur* ('The Deceiver') that was quite popular when performed in Moscow.

This was the year when she promulgated the new charters on the nobility and towns, and she also undertook a journey to inspect the important canal system through which goods were imported into St Petersburg. On this trip she was joined not just by the usual courtiers but foreign envoys too; Catherine judged that they would repay her hospitality by writing glowing reports about her and the court and boost her reputation. She was also constantly preoccupied with the development and education of her grandsons, especially the eldest whom she often referred to as 'Monsieur Alexandre'.

By the spring of 1785 Catherine had overcome her grief sufficiently to install a new favourite. He was Alexander Yermolov, yet another handsome Guards officer, tall and blond, who had been on Potemkin's staff. However, his tenure abruptly ended a year later in July 1786 when he was dismissed and sent abroad – though not before he had been given the customary land and serfs, money and of course a silver service. The reasons for his demise are unclear. It appears he had unwisely become involved in a conspiracy to oust Potemkin, using the pretext of a financial scandal said to involve the Prince. Certainly there was a cooling between Catherine and Potemkin in May 1786, though observers at the time exaggerated its importance and in any case Potemkin confidently and accurately predicted that no one would topple him. It may also be that Catherine had already fallen for her next favourite, Alexander Dmitriyev-Mamonov. He was more cultivated and cultured than his predecessor – for example Catherine was impressed by his command of French. He was also Potemkin's adjutant and a distant relative.

The replacement of Alexander Yermolov with Alexander Dmitriyev-Mamonov showed that, much to the dismay of his enemies, Potemkin's longstanding influence was as strong as ever. Though Catherine at times found him difficult, sulky, over-theatrical and jealous, she loved him deeply and emotionally as a true friend – her soulmate even – while on a political level he had the intelligence, flair, vision and boldness that she wanted in her chief advisor. Indeed Potemkin was about to play yet another important part in Catherine's reign. Ever since 1783 the Prince had wanted the Empress to visit the new lands of the Crimea that together they had conquered for Russia. For various reasons the trip had been postponed, but in early 1787 Catherine was about to make the most dramatic tour of her reign.

War, Revolution and Reaction 1787–96

Catherine's journey to see Russia's new possessions in the south was an epic affair and the convoy that left Tsarskoye Selo on 7 January 1787 must have been an impressive sight. It was made up of some 14 huge carriages plus 124 sledges – with 40 more kept in reserve – while more than 550 fresh horses met the huge travelling group at each staging post. The Empress' entourage included the ambassadors of Britain, Austria and France – her so-called 'pocket envoys' – plus senior courtiers, while there were also hundreds of servants to look after them, including apothecaries, doctors, cooks, footmen and washerwomen. Catherine's own carriage was huge and it alone needed ten horses to pull it across the frozen snow. Inside were six seats reserved for the Empress, her favourite Mamonov and her maid of honour, while the other three spaces were rotated between the senior courtiers and foreign ambassadors. All were wrapped up warm in bearskins and sables against temperatures outside that could plummet to minus 25° Celsius or lower. The convoy travelled by day, but because this was the middle of the Russian winter daylight hours were short and huge bonfires were set ablaze to light their way across the vast countryside

Despite the theatrical scale of the convoy this was a working trip. As ever the industrious Catherine kept up with her paperwork along the way, rising at 6 a.m. to work in the palaces that had been prepared for her along the way, and retiring at 9 p.m. for the same reason. At this time the Empress was working on major plans for constitutional reform in Russia, based partly on her own 'Great Instruction' and also on her own copious notes on the English jurist William Blackstone's *Commentaries on the Laws of England*. Catherine was considering the establishment of a new part-judicial, part-legislative court, with some of the characteristics of the British House of Lords. Though these ideas never became law, they show that even at this late stage, and even as she sped across Russia's frozen landscape, Catherine was still looking for new solutions to the problem of how to govern the country more effectively.

Notable absentees from the journey south were Catherine's beloved grandsons Alexander and Constantine, and the Grand Duke and Grand Duchess. The Empress had in fact ordered that the two young boys travel with them, much to the annoyance of the Grand Duke and Grand Duchess. For both personal and political reasons they did not wish to be separated from their sons for such a long time. The result was another dispute between Catherine and her son Paul, until fate intervened and Alexander fell ill, meaning he could not make the journey. Another notable absentee was Potemkin, the principle organiser of the trip, who had gone on ahead to finalise preparations.

The convoy went first to Smolensk and then reached Kiev late in January with temperatures at minus 20° C. Catherine had previously visited this ancient city back in 1744, though she was given a rather more exuberant welcome this time. The convoy had to stay in Kiev for three months until the frozen Dnieper river melted and they could navigate their way down it. Potemkin met the Empress in Kiev, and brought a guest of his, the Spanish American adventurer Francisco de Miranda, a renowned womaniser. Catherine seems to have been taken by his charms, which gave rise to unfounded rumours that they enjoyed a brief affair. There was little doubt, however, that with Miranda and the equally libidinous Potemkin

Stanislas Poniatowski, King of Poland

in town, there was a festive, almost debauched atmosphere around much of the court. However Catherine had soon grown tired of the city and was relieved when at last in late April the party could continue its journey down the Dnieper, with the Empress on board a galley named after the river.

Soon afterwards the Empress' party was greeted at Kaniv by the King of Poland, her old lover Stanilas Poniatowski, who had been waiting there patiently for three months to greet her. This was an awkward occasion. The King laid on a lavish and very costly celebration, but to his consternation he was unable to persuade Catherine to spend more than a day there. It seemed she had now little sentiment to spare for her first real love. *It was nearly thirty years since I had seen him*, she wrote later to Grimm. *And you can imagine that we found each other changed.* For his part the King may have hoped that there would still be a spark between the old lovers; the practical Catherine however had long ago moved on and was far more interested in ensuring she kept an appointment with Emperor Joseph later in the journey.[72]

Catherine eventually met Joseph on 7 May – in a field near Kaydaki – and together they travelled on to the new fortress port of Kherson, on the Dnieper and Black Sea. Afterwards, determined to impress the Austria Emperor, Catherine took him on a rapid tour of the Crimea, a trip that also included a review of the brand new Russian Black Sea fleet built up under Potemkin's guidance. The empress also took the unexpected step of officially toasting the Emperor for Austria's help in taking the Crimea. This delighted Joseph who was unaware that this gesture was quietly struck from the official record of proceedings. Catherine did not want anyone else to share in her glory, even if she did sometimes need their support. A feature of the trip before, during and after Joseph's visit had ended was the lavish and exotic celebrations staged by Potemkin, who had a real gift for such large-scale displays. They included huge firework displays, a regiment of Greek women soldiers or 'Amazons' and even a massive reconstruction using 50,000 troops of Peter the Great's historic victory over the Swedish king Charles XII at Poltava. The success of the visit and the great spectacles prompted Catherine to honour Potemkin with the epithet 'Tavrichevsky' meaning 'of the Tauride' or Crimea. It also helped to start the myth of the so-called 'Potemkin Villages'.

The Empress returned to Moscow in late June where she marked her 25 years in power and finally made it back to Tsarskoye Selo on 11 July after six months and 4,000 miles of travel. Though very weary, Catherine was delighted with the trip, in which she had been able to see much more of her empire, while her journey and meeting with Joseph had also won her considerable international standing.

Catherine had little time, however, to bask in the glory. First some unrest among workers in St Petersburg and concerns over a poor harvest worried her. Then far more seriously growing Turkish anger over Russian expansion and the growth of its fleet in the Black Sea finally came to a head. By the end of August 1787 the Ottoman Empire had once again declared war on Russia. Though the news was not entirely unexpected Catherine nonetheless wept at the thought of another conflict. There were other complications too. The man upon whom she would rely on more than ever now would of course be Potemkin. He was in charge of the army and navy, had a fine military record and knew the area and his enemy very well. Unfortunately, however, a mixture of illness and some early setbacks involving the Russian fleet sent the volatile

'Potemkin Villages' was the name given to the painted facades of villages that the Prince was reputed to have had erected along the banks of the Dnieper when Catherine passed, in order to show the prosperity of the area and boost his own prestige. They were then supposed to have been dismantled when the Empress' ship had passed and re-erected further down the river. The idea of a Potemkin Village meaning something that is sham or false thus passed into the language. In fact there is no evidence at all that Potemkin did this and the story was probably invented by a hostile foreign diplomat. Potemkin had for some years faced largely untrue accusations that he had done nothing with Russia's new possessions in the south.

Prince whirling into a fit of despair and depression. He wrote to Catherine claiming that everything had gone 'topsy-turvy', that 'God' had defeated him and that it would be better to hand over his command to someone else. He even suggested Russia should retreat from the Crimea. Catherine, however knew her man and quietly and calmly cajoled him back into the fray, even urging him to attack the Turkish forces. *I do not demand the impossible, but only write what I think*, she said in a letter to him.[73]

However, the strain was beginning to take its toll on Catherine herself, as she became prone to a series of mostly minor ailments. Indeed in April 1788 *The Time*s of London even announced her death. Meanwhile there was growing tension on another front, this time the north, with rumours that Gustavus II of Sweden, her cousin, was prepared to go to war over territorial disputes in Finland. More than ever she was missing the close guidance of Potemkin, who to make matters worse was slow in responding to letters. *I wish you were here, I would discuss matters with you for five minutes and would then decide what to do*, she wrote to him wistfully. Not for the first time the ageing Catherine was feeling the loneliness of power.[74]

By the middle of summer the Empress realised that conflict with the belligerent Gustavus was inevitable and hostilities with Sweden were officially declared on 2 July. Russia was now at war on two fronts, an uncomfortable position for any nation to be in, and the situation was made even more uneasy by the fact that the conflict in the north was close to St Petersburg itself. Yet Catherine usually thrived in a crisis and was able to write bullishly to Potemkin that *Petersburg has at this moment the look of an armed camp and I myself am like the quartermaster-general ... the smell of gunpowder was scented in town.* Some encouraging victories against the Swedes and the Turks also calmed her nerves.[75]

Potemkin's victory at Ochakov in late 1788 and the Prince's subsequent three-month stay in the capital – where he was feted and honoured by Catherine – boosted her spirits even though both wars continued. Yet there were problems looming closer to home. By early 1789 Catherine was complaining of Mamonov's coldness towards her. She was especially miserable on her 60th birthday on

21 April. Soon afterwards Catherine found out that her favourite had been in love for some months with a Princess Shcherbatova, and had even promised to marry her. It is not clear whether the Empress knew of or suspected this relationship – others at court certainly did – but in any case Catherine was upset at the news. However, once again she showed her usual generosity and lack of vindictiveness by blessing the happy couple and giving her former favourite a generous pay-off. Indeed Catherine may have been quietly preparing for this outcome, because immediately a new favourite was installed, her last and the most damaging to her reputation – yet another young officer called Platon Zubov. He was just 22, dark, handsome and was to prove very ambitious both for himself and his family.

Catherine was keen for Potemkin to approve of her new favourite, who was not a protégé of the prince, and at the same time wrote to him frankly of her infatuation with the young man. *I am fat and merry, come back to life like a fly in summer*, she declared. And when Potemkin replied that he approved, Catherine seemed grateful and relieved – though she also showed she understood something of the personality of her new favourite. *It is a great satisfaction for me, my friend, that you are pleased with me and little Blackie* [her pet name for Zubov] ... *I hope he doesn't become spoilt.*[76]

As Catherine's emotional life seemed to take a turn for the better, there was more potentially disturbing news from Europe. Catherine was at Tsarskoye Selo when she heard reports of the storming of the Bastille in France and the start of what became known as the French Revolution. Though Catherine was doubtful about Louis XVI's qualities as a monarch and quickly saw that he would not survive the crisis, she was no revolutionary and was scathing about the turn of events in France. *And how is it possible for cobblers to govern?*, she icily asked the French envoy the Comte de Ségur. And though a string of victories in the south under Potemkin pleased the Empress, 1790 was to prove another tough year. The death of Joseph II of Austria meant the loss not just of a friend but an ally too. Later in the year, meanwhile, the continuing war with Sweden came even closer to home when after some successes a Russian fleet was defeated on 28 June at Rochensalm with the loss of 6,000 men killed or captured. Once more Catherine stayed calm in the face of a setback and her coolness was rewarded when, with the Swedish advances going nowhere, the war ended as abruptly as it had started.

Under a peace agreement reached in early August both sides kept the same pre-war borders. As she wrote to Potemkin, *one paw we have pulled out of the mud, as soon as you pull out the other we'll sing alleluia.*[77]

Following events in France Catherine was more sensitive than ever about criticism or unrest at home. She was therefore outraged at the publication of a book – passed by her official censor – which had the seemingly innocuous title *A Journey from St Petersburg to Moscow*. This was no innocent travelogue, however, but in Catherine's eyes an attack by the anonymous author on Russia, its government and especially her. She described its author as being *infected and full of the French madness ... trying in every way possible to break down respect for authority and the authorities.* In fact the author was an educated nobleman called Alexander Radishchev, whose studies abroad had in part been funded by Catherine and the crown. In many ways he was the kind of thoughtful, enlightened and educated nobleman

A formal system of censorship did not exist in Russia under Catherine until 1796, the last year of her life. Up until then censorship had generally been a rather haphazard affair. Ironically in 1789 Radishchev had taken advantage of a 1783 law allowing individuals to set up a printing press to publish his offending title. Local police chiefs were supposed to read material printed on such presses to ensure that they did not attack the Empress, the church or public morals, though in practice censorship of this kind could be quite lax. However, after the French Revolution and the execution of Louis XVI censorship was enforced more rigorously, culminating in a new system in 1796.

whose development Catherine had encouraged and had felt that Russia needed in order to become more modern and open to new ideas.

However, with Russia at war and French society in revolt, this was not a good time to test Catherine's patience with challenging criticism. The unfortunate Radishchev was arrested and subsequently sentenced to death, though this was later commuted to losing all rank and being sent to Siberia. It was not so much that Catherine was becoming more illiberal – she had never been a liberal anyway. It was more that that the inherent contractions that she had dimly seen between her absolute monarchism and some of the Enlightenment ideals – for example during her conversations with Diderot – were now being brought sharply into focus by the unfolding of events in France, the spiritual home of Enlightenment thinking.[78]

Early in 1791 Potemkin returned once more to St Petersburg, the war in the south again in winter limbo. On the surface all seemed well and his arrival was feted. But there were underlying strains in the relationship between the Prince and his Empress. The British and the Prussians had become alarmed at Russia's ambitions in and around the Black Sea and were threatening military action. Catherine and Potemkin fell out over the best policy to adopt, with the Empress unwilling to give way to the Anglo-Prussian threats while Potemkin was worried about Russia being at war with Britain, Prussia and Poland as well as the Ottoman Empire. The tensions were heightened by the fact that Zubov's influence was growing and that he was scheming against the Prince. Potemkin in turn hoped to be able to topple the new favourite or at least curb his growing power. In fact the British threats subsided when Prime Minister William Pitt came under domestic pressure over a policy of supporting the Ottoman Empire against a fellow European Christian power. In Britain this was known as the Ochakov Crisis. Slowly the crisis faded in Russia too.

Yet the tensions between Catherine and Potemkin remained, even though the latter staged an elaborate celebration at his St Petersburg palace that delighted the Empress. Catherine, egged on by Zubov, had begun to worry at Potemkin's domineering behaviour, while others thought he had simply gone mad. Up to now the Empress and her Prince had had an almost identical view of foreign policy but this had no longer been the case during the Ochakov affair. On one occasion the Empress is said to have told Potemkin: *We were running things all right without you, weren't we?* However, despite this, and the serious rows the pair had, there is no real sign that Potemkin had seriously lost the confidence of the Empress or that the Prince was on his way out, to be replaced by the far less competent Zubov. Indeed when Potemkin finally left St Petersburg on 24 July 1791, galloping south to try to make peace with the Turks, Catherine sent a note after him which said *Goodbye my friend, I kiss you.* Perhaps she knew then that she would never see her Prince again.[79]

The death of Prince Potemkin on a desolate hillside in the Bessarabian steppe near Jassy (now Iasi in Romania) on 5 October 1791 did not come as a huge surprise to Catherine, as he had been fighting illness for some weeks after his departure. This did not stop her being utterly devastated. The man with whom she had shared the hopes, dreams and achievements of Russia had gone. In a letter to Grimm she showed how much Potemkin had meant to her, whatever their recent disagreements. Describing him as her *my pupil, my friend, and almost my idol*, Catherine said his *most rare quality was a courage of heart, mind and soul which distinguished him completely from the rest of humankind and which meant that we understood one another perfectly . . I regard Prince Potemkin as a very great man* . . .[80] Potemkin had indeed been a great man, even if his reputation was later sullied by enemies and those who were envious of his great influence. If it had been Grigory Orlov who had helped Catherine become empress, it had been Grigory Potemkin who had helped Catherine become a great ruler. She would miss him greatly for the remainder of her life.

Before his demise Potemkin had begun a peace process which resulted in a treaty with the Turks in January 1792. Even this was a bitter reminder of the Prince's death and when on 30 January the Prince's nephew General Alexander Samoilov arrived with the Turks' ratification, Catherine and the General closeted themselves away alone to shed tears for him. However, as the conscientious Catherine knew, government had to continue and inevitably Zubov's status and powers grew. Indeed nearly all of the old faces that had surrounded Catherine for so long, and had mostly served her so well, were now making way for new people. This included the stalwart Procurator-General Alexander Viazemskii who had been one of the Empress' most shrewd appointments but who by 1792 had become frail and unable to do work properly. He was replaced by Samoilov.

Growing concern in Catherine about the situation in revolutionary France was reflected both in her surveillance of French nationals in Russia and her worry about plots to either assassinate her or spread discontent. In April 1792 the Empress started an inquiry into the prevalence of Freemasonry – something Catherine had always mistrusted – in Moscow. It led to the arrest of a nobleman, a publisher and mason called Nikolai Novikov, who was later sentenced to 15 years imprisonment. The investigation appeared to show that freemasons were keen to get the Grand Duke Paul – with whom Catherine's relations were as bad as ever – to join their number, even though he denied any involvement. It was an unnerving time to be an absolute monarch in Europe.

Though attempts at matchmaking for her grandson Alexander – who was 15 in December 1792 – briefly lifted Catherine's spirits, this did not last long. Early in the next year reports reached the Empress of Louis XVI's execution. This news horrified her to such an extent that it made her physically ill and she retired to her bed, while ordering measures to be taken against French nationals and goods. Then in early spring the now seriously overweight Catherine tumbled down 15 steps, an incident that both scared her and left her with a permanently weak knee.

By this time Russia and Prussia had already carried out what is known as the Second Partition of Poland, ostensibly in the name of defending themselves against 'Jacobinism' or revolution. This act was a sign of Catherine's ruthlessness when it came to what she saw as Russian's national interests, and also of her opportunism. Two years later in 1795 Russia took part in the Third Partition which effectively wiped Poland off the map and gave Catherine and her country considerable new territories to the west. The Empress was to be very generous in awarding land from her new territories to favourites, courtiers and other nobles

In May 1793 Catherine was buoyed by the betrothal of her beloved Alexander to his future bride Princess Louisa Augusta of Baden-Durlach, now Elizaveta Alexeyevna. More than ever Catherine saw her well-educated grandson as the future of the imperial throne. Later the same year Alexander and his bride were married at a ceremony that Paul, the bridegroom's father, almost boycotted. It was yet another sign of his estrangement from the Empress, a relationship not helped by Zubov's own evident scorn for the Grand Duke.[81] Catherine received another boost when the Russian senate, on behalf of the people, offered Catherine the formal titles of Mother of the Fatherland and the Great. Flattered and delighted though she was, she did not formally accept the titles, though she did not directly reject them either.

An unwelcome reminder of Catherine's age came in February 1794 which marked the 50th anniversary of her arrival in Russia. Now aged 64, Catherine told Grimm that with the exception of the very frail Ivan Betskoy (who had had an affair with her mother) and a handful of others, no one around her at court celebrations would be able to recall her arrival. *All the rest could be my children or my children's children. That's how aged I am*, she wrote gloomily.

The Alexander Palace was designed by Quarenghi and built by Catherine II for her grandson the future Emperor Alexander I

Meanwhile she had already asked Grimm to stop buying art on her behalf so that Russia could start to restore its badly-depleted finances. Yet another sign of her age and her changing perspectives after events in France was a new reluctance to defend old friends such as Voltaire and Diderot, whose ideas she now began to think had led to *destruction*.[82]

Her favourite Zubov, meanwhile was growing in strength and power, as were members of his family. In August 1795, for example, he was awarded more than 13,000 serfs from the new territories in Poland. Unlike most other favourites Zubov had acquired real political power as well as influence, and now there was no one such as Potemkin to stand up to him. Within the space of a few years he had become the most powerful man in Russia, and Catherine increasingly relied on him as her own health failed.

Catherine's Russia

By late 1795 Catherine, now 66, was suffering from phlebitis or inflammation of the veins and was in near-constant discomfort from swollen legs. Sometimes she even had open sores on her legs and suffered too from constant cold and aches. Yet nonetheless Catherine could still cut an impressive figure at court, even in the opinion of one young Polish nobleman Adam Czartoryski who with some cause regarded the Empress as the destroyer of his country. Though he also described her as 'very fat', Czartoryski recorded how at court 'her gait, her bearing, in fact her whole person bore the stamp of dignity and elegance ... she had no sudden movements, everything about her was grave and noble; but she was like a river that swept all before her.' Catherine's combination of dignity and informality was one of her great qualities and helped her both put people at their ease and impress them at the same time. Meanwhile the Empress' human side was reflected in her touching comments to Grimm about the decrepit Betskoy who had finally died at the age of 93. *He tried above all to hide from me the loss of his sight, so that I would not remove any of his posts from him,* she wrote. *In fact all his offices were filled but he didn't know it.*[83]

Amid these disturbing signs of ageing and decay, Catherine was still looking ahead. Though her plans to put her second grandson on the throne of a new Greek Empire were little more than a distant dream now, the Empress still showed an interest in young Constantine's future. In October 1795 she invited Princess

A full portrait of Catherine the Great

Augusta of Saxe-Coburg with her three young daughters to St Petersburg and the 16-year-old Constantine was allowed to pick which of the three young women he preferred. He chose Juliana, who was just 14 – and also the one his grandmother had preferred.

By early February 1796 she had converted to Orthodoxy with the new name of Anna Fedorovna, and by the middle of the month the young couple were married.

There was more good news over the future health of the imperial throne when in June Paul's wife Maria gave birth to her third son, a robust child who was christened Nikolai – or Nicholas as he was known in the West. Meanwhile Catherine, though she clearly still expected to reign for some years yet, was apparently giving close thought to who should succeed her. The Empress feared for Russia's future (and also her legacy) under Paul, who lived isolated from a court life whose reputation for dissipation he disliked, and who remained fascinated by military life. With him at the helm, Russia would become little more than a Prussian province, Catherine believed. She is said to have tried and failed to get the Grand Duchess to sign a document preventing her husband from acceding to the throne. Catherine also made attempts to persuade Alexander that he should be her successor. However, Alexander had no interest at that time in ruling Russia. Catherine, whose great virtue had always been her ability to read people, was sadly blind to the fact that her favourite grandson felt increasingly alienated from her and had little desire to rule. Thanks in part to his relatively liberal education – provided for by Catherine – he had grown to dislike the opulence of court and the concept of favouritism. He also had no wish to harm his father's interests. She was equally unaware that Constantine, who had a cruel streak, was frequently rude about her behind her back.[84]

Catherine's love of matchmaking continued into 1796 with attempts to marry her eldest granddaughter Alexandra to the 17-year-old King of Sweden, Gustavus Adolphus IV, whose uncle was ruling as regent until the young man reached his majority. This proposed match had the dual diplomatic aims of trying to wean Sweden away from its alliance with France while at the same time helping to prevent future wars with her Nordic neighbour. The

Empress had been furious when the young King's engagement to Princess Louisa of Mecklenberg-Schwerin had been announced the year before, but Catherine had managed to have this agreement put on hold. So when the young Swede and his entourage came to the Russian court in August 1796 there was every prospect of being able to unite two royal families. This seemed even more likely when the good-looking young prince seemed to take an instant liking to Alexandra. Catherine, who despite the political importance of it wanted her granddaughter to be happy with the match, also seems to have approved of the young King – at least at first. *He is a very distinguished figure, he is majestic and gentle … assuredly no throne in Europe can currently boast anything like as much hope*, she wrote to Grimm.[85]

However, just when it seemed that an agreement was imminent, the betrothal hit a serious snag. From the start one area of potential disagreement had been the question of religion. Gustavus was after all a Lutheran while Alexandra had been brought up in the Russian Orthodox church. Catherine was adamant that Alexandra had to be allowed to keep her faith and though Gustavus had been unhappy at this, he appeared to give his verbal consent that his future wife would have the freedom to worship as she chose. However, when the time came to sign an agreement just before the couple were to become betrothed, Russian officials noticed that the clause on religious freedom was missing. The King himself had removed it. During hours of haggling Catherine and others attempted to persuade him to sign an agreement on freedom of religion for Alexandra. He stubbornly refused, insisting he had given his verbal assurance that his bride would be free to follow her own faith and that was enough and all he would or could provide. Eventually, late into the evening the betrothal ceremony was called off with Catherine using the excuse that she was feeling ill.

Though a few days later an agreement was indeed finally signed, subject to the King giving his assent when he reached the age of 18, this was merely a face-saving exercise by the diplomats. Everyone, Catherine included, realised that the engagement was almost certainly off; as indeed it proved to be. The failure to arrange the betrothal had been a humiliating experience for the Russian court and for Catherine personally. Here was an experienced, worldly-wise empress whose plans had been thwarted by a 17-year-old. Not surprisingly the Empress' views about the young Swedish king had now changed dramatically. It also transpired that when Gustavus was thought to have been whispering affection in Alexandra's ears at court events, he had in fact been attempting to convert her to his faith.

One report at the time claimed that Catherine suffered a mild stroke during the trauma of this diplomatic shambles. It was certainly a situation that would never have been allowed to happen in the days of her earlier senior officials such as Alexander Viazemskii. Zubov may have acquired many of the powers of Catherine's previous officials but he did not match them in competence. What he did not lack, however, was self-belief. Early in 1796 he had been made a prince of the Holy Roman Empire, a coveted title that Potemkin had also been given. He was even emboldened enough to make amorous overtures to Alexander's wife Elizaveta, until Catherine had to warn him about his behaviour. Zubov's stock rose even higher when Catherine agreed to send his brother Valerian with a small force into Persian territory along the Caspian Sea. This was another attempt by Catherine to emulate Peter the Great's own Persian campaign of 1722.

For a while after the Swedish fiasco Catherine was little seen around the court. Once again, however, she made unsuccessful attempts to win over a reluctant Alexander to agree to become her successor, who seems to have deflected her aim with polite but vague thanks for her concern for him and his future. Catherine probably felt she still had time to win over Alexander to her plans. Publicly at least Paul remained the Empress' official successor.[86]

Catherine's last appearance in public was on 2 November 1796. Afterwards she spent two days working quietly in her private rooms, as she often liked to do. On 5 November, according to her staff, she had got up as usual in the Winter Palace, drank some black coffee and then settled down to work. After a while she went to the water closet. When she did not return her valet Zakhar Zotov went to search for her and found her slumped on the floor. Within minutes she had lapsed into unconsciousness and several servants were needed to move the 67-year-old Catherine into her bedroom where she was laid on a mattress on the floor. Her bulk made it too difficult to heave her onto the bed. The physician Dr Rogerson was called and he bled her; however it was clear to him and other court doctors that the Empress was dying. Immediately court officials sent for Paul and the Grand Duchess who were at Gatchina. Interestingly when the official messenger Nicholas Zubov – another brother of the favourite – arrived in an obvious hurry, Paul's first reaction was that he was about to be arrested. Then, informed instead of his mother's condition, the Grand Duke and his wife rushed to be by her side.

Paul stayed in a nearby room close to the dying Empress through the night, and the next day gave orders for her study to be locked and her papers sealed inside. It is widely believed it was at this time that a document supposedly drawn up by Catherine removing Paul from the succession was destroyed. The Empress, who never regained consciousness, was meanwhile slowly slipping away. She was given the last rites on the afternoon of 6 November and at 9.45 p.m. that day Catherine finally died – a post mortem examination later showing she had suffered a severe stroke. The long and eventful reign of Catherine II that had begun back in 1762 was finally over.[87]

The change of mood that greeted Paul's succession as Emperor was quickly apparent. Even before Catherine had died Alexander and Constantine had been seen around the Winter Palace in the Prussian style of uniform that had until then could only be worn at Paul and Maria's estate at Pavlosk or at Gatchina. Now Paul gave orders that, even while his mother's corpse was honoured and prepared for burial, the body of his long-dead father Peter III be dug up, his remains honoured, and then brought to the Winter Palace. By now Paul would have learnt from Catherine's private correspondence the role that Alexei Orlov had played in his father's murder. Paul therefore commanded that Orlov himself should carry his late father's imperial crown in the solemn and elaborate procession to the palace. Orlov is said to have wept upon receiving this unhappy order, but carried out his grim task with stoicism and some dignity. Peter's coffin was laid next to his former wife's, and there they stayed side by side on public display for two days until they were taken for burial at the Cathedral of Peter and Paul on 5 December. The new Emperor also ordered that while the birth and burial dates of Peter III and Catherine were put on their tomb, the dates of their deaths were omitted. Official mourning was also declared not just for Catherine II but also for Peter III. To an unknowing observer it would have looked as if the pair had ruled together all those years.[88]

The brief reign of Paul I (1754–1801) ended when he was murdered by conspirators, who strangled him in his bedroom after trying to force him to abdicate. Paul's high-handed manner and attempt to militarise them had alienated many of the nobility who were behind the plot. One of the conspirators was Catherine's former favourite Platon Zubov. Paul had despised what he had seen as the moral laxness of Catherine's court and had also called an immediate halt to her campaign in Persia. He was succeeded by his son Alexander, who was in the palace when the Emperor was assassinated.

Paul's spite against his mother was also reflected in other actions. Several towns that had been named in honour of her triumphs were renamed and the Zubovs were all banned from high office, even if Platon was not banished; Paul even helped him acquire a house in St Petersburg. Men such as Radishchev and Novikov whom Catherine had punished were released from captivity and exile. The new ruler also changed the rules of accession ensuring that from then on only men would rule Russia. However, as his mother had foreseen for many years, Paul was temperamentally unsuited to be emperor and his reign was short; and he met, as he had himself feared, a violent end.

In her lifetime Catherine had rejected the title 'the Great', though when the Senate had offered it to her a few years before her death she had been genuinely delighted. However, though she was very proud of her achievements – especially her foreign policy in the Black Sea and her Enlightenment-based reforms of Russian administration – Catherine knew that posterity would be the real judge of her reign. The modest mock epitaph she once wrote for herself perhaps understates how she really wanted to be regarded. Part of it read: *Arrived on the throne of Russia, she desired its good and sought to procure for her subjects happiness, liberty and propriety. She forgave easily and hated no one; indulgent, easy to live with, naturally cheerful, with a republican soul, and a good heart, she had friends; she found work easy, she liked good society and the arts.*[89]

The Empress was often referred to as Catherine the Great during her lifetime and despite – or perhaps even because of – Paul's attempts to discredit his mother that tag persisted and grew more widespread after her death. The historian Karamzin, writing during the reign of her grandson Alexander I, felt able to praise Catherine's rule in lavish terms even if he shared Alexander's disapproval of the morals of her court. He wrote that 'should we compare all the known epochs of Russian history, virtually all would agree that Catherine's epoch was the happiest for Russian citizens'.[90]

There were other contemporaries, too, who praised Catherine.

For example Princess Dashkova, who had been close to Catherine at the time of her accession, even if their relationship had not always remained so warm, compared her favourably with that giant of recent Russia history Peter the Great. Not long after her death an anonymous British observer praised Catherine's 'extraordinary talents' and the fact that she was a 'perfect mistress of all her passions' even if he was critical of her military campaigns.

Yet many commentators both then and afterwards were not so kind about the Empress and her reign. The great Russian poet Alexander Pushkin, writing in the 19th century, dismissed her as a hypocrite. Indeed this became a theme for many subsequent writers who have suggested that Catherine's long correspondence with the philosophers of the day, her reading of the great Enlightenment works, her 'Great Instruction' and her attempts at reform were simply diversions to disguise the fact that she was an absolute monarch who cared little for her subjects and their well-being.[91]

The idea of a powerful female ruler has often gripped the imagination of writers, and the example of Catherine II is no exception. George Bernard Shaw wrote the play *Great Catherine: A Thumbnail Sketch of Russian Court Life in the XVIII Century* which was first performed in 1913. This largely sympathetic portrayal in turn inspired a number of films. In various movies Catherine was portrayed by Jeanne Moreau, Bette Davis, Marlene Dietrich and Tallulah Bankhead. In 1944 the actress Mae West had a hit with a stage production called *Catherine Was Great* which gave a warm and sympathetic view of the Empress.

However, much of the criticism that Catherine has suffered has centred on her personal life, her system of favourites and especially on her supposed fondness for sex. The allegedly lax morals of her court were certainly disapproved of by her grandson Alexander and by Pushkin. But even before she died, Catherine's predilection for young officers as her favourites had provoked mirth and scorn across parts of Europe, as well as more discreetly in Russia itself, for example among Freemasons

Of the many cinematic portrayals of Catherine the Great few rival that of Marlene Dietrich in *The Scarlet Empress* in 1934

and sections of the Russian Orthodox Church. During the so-called Ochakov Crisis of 1791 satirical engravings and drawings in England and France made much of Catherine's supposed appetite for sex. In one the Sultan of Turkey is seen to exclaim that 'The Whole Turkish Army wouldn't satisfy her'. Then a few months after her death the great English Romantic poet Samuel Taylor Coleridge set the tone for much subsequent opinion on her private life in his poem 'Ode on the departing year'.

'No more on Murder's lurid face/The insatiate Hag shall gloat with drunken eye!' wrote the poet. Stories about Catherine and sex have fascinated and titillated ever since.

The most infamous and baseless story about her is the absurd one about Catherine's supposed sexual taste for horses and how this apparently led to her death. The origins of this strange invention may be linked to a ribald old Russian poem about a character called Luka the Horse, 18th-century stories in the West of alleged Russian bestiality and Catherine's own undoubted ability as a horsewoman. In fact, though Catherine seems to have enjoyed a perfectly normal sex life with her lovers, what she most craved from her favourites appears to have been to love and be loved. It should also be noted that what was regarded by some as shocking behaviour on Catherine's part – having a succession of young favourites or lovers – would have been regarded as normal or even praiseworthy in a male ruler. What is true is that even if on the surface it practiced decorum and decency, Catherine's court was a place full of sexual intrigue and dalliances. Not only were men such as Grigory Orlov and Prince Potemkin noted for their many liaisons, so too were trusted officials such as Alexander Viazemskii and Alexander Bezborodko. Observers living in the more outwardly moral and puritanical 19th century often looked back with disdain upon such behaviour.[92]

The attention focussed on Catherine II's private life has often obscured the Empress' many real achievements. The most obvious of these was her extension of Russia's borders to the south and the fact that Catherine's policies led to Russia achieving her historic objective of gaining access to the Black Sea. This was a policy that Catherine followed with determination and vision, supported by men such as Grigory Orlov and above all Potemkin. Her achievements in reaching the Black Sea surpassed the efforts of even her great hero and predecessor Peter the Great. In contrast her major role in the partition and eventual obliteration of Poland was a blot on her reign, as were the deaths of her husband Peter III and the former emperor Ivan VI. Catherine was undoubtedly both ambitious and at times ruthless.

Closer to home, Catherine carried out major reforms of government, courts and the organisation of towns, as well as taking practical measures over health, welfare and education. Many of these, for example her establishment of a state education system, did have lasting value even if historians often debate their precise legacy. Certainly, like Peter the Great before her, Catherine sought to modernise Russia, though she was far more pragmatic than him and always carefully weighed up the likely impact of proposed changes. Catherine also sought to make the state more just as well as more efficient. Although as she grew older she herself understood the growing gap between the ideals of Enlightenment thinking and the practical constraints of governing a country as vast as Russia, this did not stop her trying to bring enlightened values of social justice into government and into the law. She has often been criticised for improving the lot of the nobility but not of the serfs, even though she was sympathetic to their plight. In fact the Empress did try to reduce the ways in which people could be made serfs and also increased the security of those who had been freed. Yet she also realised that Russia and its old traditional structures was simply not then capable of dealing with a major reform of the status of serfs.

Alexander I (1777–1825) became Emperor after the murder of his father Paul. He was greatly influenced by the tutor that his grandmother Catherine had given him, the liberally-inclined Swiss thinker Frédéric César de La Harpe who preached the virtues of private and public morality. The early part of Alexander's reign was marked by relatively progressive measures. However, he is best known for having successfully resisted the invasion of Napoleon Bonaparte in 1812. Nicholas (1796–1855) became Emperor in 1825 when Alexander died without producing a legitimate male heir – his older brother Constantine had already renounced the throne. Nicholas codified Russian law and continued his grandmother's and brothers' policy of expansion in the south, leading to the Crimean War in 1853. He was succeeded by his son Alexander II.

Like her hero Peter the Great Catherine also succeeded in making Russia a major player in European affairs. This was not just in the military and diplomatic sense, but also in terms of trade, the arts and culture. Catherine's patronage of the arts, her collections of paintings, sculptures and books, her encouragement of architecture, garden design, and new writing, plus the splendour of her court made Russia in general and St Petersburg in particular a significant cultural player in European affairs. The world-renowned Hermitage Museum in St Petersburg began as Catherine's own collection. And despite the criticism, Catherine genuinely was interested in ideas and philosophy, as well as more widely in the arts and in design. Though she was certainly keen for the rest of Europe to have a favourable impression of both Russia and her, and though she understood the importance of image, Catherine's interest in such subjects was not feigned. In her love of ideas, books and the arts, she was very much a child of her age.

One of her greatest achievements, perhaps, was in her style of government. This was a woman who had actively prepared herself for government and was determined to make the most of the resources at her disposal. In particular, Catherine had an ability to spot great talent in others and then allow them to get on with their work, though always under her supervision. This meant that men of such prodigious talent as Potemkin and the rather more understated Viazemskii were allowed to make their mark on Russian life. Her aptitude for hard work, her encouragement of objective and non-sycophantic advice and her attention to detail all contrasted strongly with many of the rulers who preceded and followed her, as did her encouragement of a civilian administration as opposed to one that was entirely subservient to the military. The resurgence of a military ethos in the Russian court under Paul and later emperors underlines the rare importance of this achievement. Catherine also showed a restraint and lack of vengefulness towards opponents as well as a kindness towards those who worked for her that was quite remarkable for the age.

Of course, as she grew older and the political climate in Europe

The foundation of the art collection in the Hermitage Museum, in St Petersburg, is Catherine the Great's most precious legacy

changed, some of her tolerance was qualified by fear of unrest and rebellion. She undoubtedly found it ever harder to reconcile the conflicting demands of Enlightenment ideals and the practical problems of autocratic government. Yet set against the chaos of much of the 17th century and the grim days that lay ahead in the 19th century for Russian rulers, Catherine's rule stands out for its ambition to do good, its calmness and a spirit of moderation, qualities that stemmed from the ruler herself. Many years before she died the British envoy to St Petersburg Sir James Harris had noted that: 'In an absolute monarchy everything depends on the disposition and character of the Sovereign'.[93] It was fortunate for Russia in the second half of the 18th century that it was able to depend on the character of an ambitious young German princess who went on to become one of the most remarkable rulers in that country's history.

Notes

1. This date, 21 April 1729, is according to the old style Julian Calendar that was used in Russia at this time. This calendar was at that time 11 days behind the Gregorian Calendar introduced by Pope Gregory XIII in 1582 and which was by the early 18th century was widespread in much of Europe (though it was not introduced in England until 1752). In the Gregorian calendar Sophia was born on 2 May 1729.

2. *Zapiski Imperatritsky Ekateriny Vtoroi* (Spb., 1907), 15; quoted in John T Alexander, *Catherine The Great* (Oxford University Press, Oxford: 1989) pp 21–2.

3. Dominique Maroger, translated by Moura Budberg, *The Memoirs of Catherine The Great* (Hamish Hamilton, London: 1955) p 29, hereafter Maroger.

4. Mark Cruise and Hilde Hoogenboom (translators), *The Memoirs of Catherine the Great* (Random House, New York: 2005) pp 4–5, hereafter Cruise and Hoogenboom.

5. See Alexander, *Catherine the Great*, pp 21–2; also Carolly Erickson, *Great Catherine, The Life of Catherine the Great, Empress of Russia* (Robson, London: 1994) pp 21–2.

6. For a discussion of this affair see: Isabel de Madariaga, *Russia in the age of Catherine the Great* (Weidenfeld and Nicolson, London: 1982) p 4; Alexander, *Catherine the Great*, pp 22–3; Virginia Rounding, *Catherine the Great, Love, Sex*

and Power (Hutchinson, London: 2006) pp 15 –17, hereafter Rounding.

7. Maroger, p 60.
8. Cruise and Hoogenboom, p 9.
9. Cruise and Hoogenboom, pp 22–3.
10. Cruise and Hoogenboom, p 7 and pp 9–10.
11. Cruise and Hoogenboom, pp 31–2.
12. Maroger, p 80.
13. Cruise and Hoogenboom, pp 32–4.
14. Cruise and Hoogenboom, p 41.
15. Cruise and Hoogenboom, p 48.
16. Cruise and Hoogenboom, p 50.
17. Cruise and Hoogenboom, pp 81–4; see also Alexander, *Catherine the Great*, pp 41–2.
18. Maroger, p 203.
19. Cruise and Hoogenboom, p 146.
20. Quoted in Alexander, *Catherine the Great*, p 48.
21. The Earl of Ilchester and Mrs Langford-Brooke, *Correspondence of Catherine the Great when Grand Duchess with Sir Charles Hanbury-Williams and letters from Count Poniatowski* (Thornton Butterworth Ltd, London: 1928) p 90; p 45.
22. Cruise and Hoogenboom, p 207; On Elizabeth's plans see Alexander, *Catherine the Great*, p 48.
23. Maroger, p 329.
24. Maroger, p 330.
25. Maroger, p 338.
26. A Lentin, *Russia in the Eighteenth Century, from Peter the Great to Catherine the Great* (Heinemann, London: 1973) pp 68–70.
27. Maroger, p 341.
28. V A Bil'basov, *Istoriia Ekateriny Vtoroi* (Berlin: 1900) Vol 2 pp 97–9, hereafter Bil'basov; quoted in Alexander, *Catherine the Great*, p 8.

29. Bil'basov, Vol 2, p 137; quoted in Alexander, *Catherine the Great*, p 11.

30. Madariaga, *Russia in the age of Catherine the Great*, p 32.

31. *Sbornik imperatorskago russkago istoricheskago obshchestva*, Vol 7 p 346, hereafter SIRIO.

32. David L Ransel, *The Politics of Catherinian Russia: The Panin Party* (Yale University Press, Yale: 1925) p 125.

33. SIRIO, Vol 7, p 365.

34. Aleksandr Nikolaevich Pypin (ed), *Sochineniia Imperatritsy Ekateriny II* (St Petersburg: 1901–07) Vol VII, pp 524–5; Madariaga, *Russia in the age of Catherine the Great*, p 151; Lentin, *Russia in the Eighteenth Century*, p 84; Alexander, *Catherine the Great*, p 101.

35. For a discussion of this see Madariaga, *Russia in the age of Catherine the Great*, pp 151–63.

36. SIRIO, Vol 10, pp 170–1.

37. SIRIO, Vol 10, p 204.

38. SIRIO, Vol 10, p 235; see for example Alexander, *Catherine the Great*, pp 112–20; Madariaga, *Russia in the age of Catherine the Great*, pp 164–83.

39. SIRIO, Vol 7, pp 373–4; see also Madariaga, *Russia in the age of Catherine the Great*, pp 196–204.

40. W Richardson, Anecdotes of the Russian Empire (Strahan & Cadell, London: 1784) pp 19–20.

41. W F Reddaway (ed), *Documents of Catherine the Great: The Correspondence with Voltaire and the Instruction of 1767 in the English Text of 1768* (Cambridge University Press, Cambridge: 1931) p 32, hereafter Reddaway.

42. Reddaway, pp 74–6; see also Alexander, *Catherine the Great*, pp 132–3.

43. SIRIO, Vol 10, pp 180, 186; see also Alexander, *Catherine the Great*, pp 103–05.

44. A Lentin (ed), *Voltaire and Catherine the Great; selected correspondence* (Cambridge University Press, Cambridge: 1974) pp 99–100; SIRIO, Vol 13, p 59.

45. Madariaga, *Russia in the age of Catherine the Great*, pp 337–8.

46. Lentin (ed), *Voltaire and Catherine the Great; selected correspondence*, p 78.

47. Lentin (ed), *Voltaire and Catherine the Great; selected correspondence*, p 122.

48. Lentin (ed), *Voltaire and Catherine the Great; selected correspondence*, p 122.

49. Simon Sebag Montefiore, *Potemkin: Catherine the Great's Imperial Partner* (Vintage, London: 2005) p 91; SIRIO, Vol 13, p 258, hereafter Sebag Montefiore.

50. SIRIO, Vol 13, p 348.

51. SIRIO, Vol 13, pp 332–6.

52. Sebag Montefiore, p 93

53. Douglas Smith (ed and trans), *Love & Conquest: Personal Correspondence of Catherine the Great and Prince Grigory Potemkin* (Northern Illinois University Press, DeKalb: 2004) pp 18–19.

54. Sebag Montefiore, pp 110–11, 114–15; Rounding, p 272.

55. SIRIO, Vol 19, pp 405–07.

56. Alexander, *Catherine the Great*, p 173; Isabel de Madariaga, 'Catherine the Great and the Philosophes' in A G Cross (ed), *Russia and the West in the Eighteenth Century* (Newtonville, Massasachussetts: 1983) pp 38–47.

57. Lentin (ed), *Voltaire and Catherine the Great; selected correspondence*, p 164.

58. John T Alexander, *Autocratic Politics in a National Crisis: The Imperial Russian Government and Pugachev's Revolt, 1773-1775* (Bloomington, Indiana: 1969) pp 203–05.

59. Sebag Montefiore, p 135.

60. SIRIO, Vol 23, p 13.

61. Sebag Montefiore pp 147, 152–4, 159.
62. Public Records Office, State papers (London) 91/102:311-312, quoted in Alexander, *Catherine the Great*, p 215.
63. SIRIO, Vol 23, p 93.
64. See Madariaga, *Russia in the age of Catherine the Great*, pp 532–48.
65. Madariaga, *Russia in the age of Catherine the Great*, p 354; SIRIO, Vol 23, p 107; Rounding, pp 329, 346–7.
66. SIRIO, Vol 23, pp 183–4; Alexander, *Catherine the Great*, p 243.
67. SIRIO, Vol 9, pp 158–9; Alexander, *Catherine the Great*, pp 245–6.
68. For a full analysis see Madariaga, *Russia in the age of Catherine the Great*, pp 292–307 and pp 488–502.
69. SIRIO, Vol 23, pp 268, 274–5; Alexander, *Catherine the Great*, p 255.
70. SIRIO, Vol 27, pp 221–8.
71. SIRIO, Vol 27, p 244; Alexander, *Catherine the Great*, p 217.
72. SIRIO, Vol 23, p 408; see also Rounding, pp 432–4.
73. Sebag Montefiore. pp 386–7; SIRIO, Vol 27, p 424.
74. Quoted in Rounding, pp 442–3.
75. SIRIO, Vol 27, pp 512–13.
76. Sebag Montefiore, pp 424–5.
77. SIRIO, Vol 42, pp 99, 101; see Alexander, *Catherine the Great*, p 279.
78. See Alexander, pp 282–5.
79. Quoted in Sebag Montefiore, pp 474, 479; see Alexander, *Catherine the Great*, pp 286–8 on Potemkin's mental state as well as Sebag Montefiore, pp 467–79.
80. SIRIO, Vol 23, p 561; see also Rounding, pp 464–5.
81. Alexander, *Catherine the Great*, p 311; see also Rounding. pp 475–6.

82. SIRIO, Vol 23, pp 592–3; Alexander, *Catherine the Great*, p 312; Rounding, p 477.

83. Prince A Czartoryski, *Mémoires* (Plon, Paris: 1887) Vol I, pp 68–9; SIRIO, Vol 23, pp 644–5; see also Rounding, pp 481–3.

84. Alexander, *Catherine the Great*, p 322; Madariaga, *Russia in the age of Catherine the Great*, pp 570–7.

85. SIRIO, Vol 23, pp 691–2.

86. Madariaga, *Russia in the age of Catherine the Great*, pp 576–7.

87. Madariaga, *Russia in the age of Catherine the Great*, p 578; Rounding, pp 499–502; Alexander, *Catherine the Great*, pp 324–5.

88. Rounding, p 504.

89. SIRIO, Vol 23, p 77, quoted in Rounding, p 505.

90. Quoted in Madariaga, *Russia in the age of Catherine the Great*, p 581.

91. E R Dashovoa, ed and trans Kyril Fitzlyon, *The Memoirs of Princess Dashkov* (London: 1958) pp 286–8; quoted in Alexander, *Catherine the Great*, pp 330–1; Madariaga, *Russia in the age of Catherine the Great*, pp 581–8.

92. Quoted in Alexander, *Catherine the Great*, pp 289, 331, and see pp 332–5 for a serious discussion of the origins of the horse story; see also Rounding, p 508.

93. For a discussion of her legacy see Madariaga, *Russia in the age of Catherine the Great*, pp 581–8; quoted at: Isabel de Madariaga, *Catherine the Great: a Short History* (Yale University, New Haven and London: 1990) p 203.

Year	Age	Life
1729		29 April: Sophia Augusta Fredericka, Princess of Anhalt-Zerbst born at Stettin, Pomerania, to parents Prince Christian August and Princess Johanna Elizabeth.
1739	10	First meets future husband, Duke Peter Karl Ulrich of Holstein at Eutin.
1744	14	January: Sophia and mother invited to Russia by Empress Elizabeth. *En route* to Russia, meets Frederick II (The Great) in Berlin. February: Arrives Moscow to meet Empress Elizabeth. June: Converts to Orthodox church, takes name Catherine.
1745	16	21 August: Marries Grand Duke Peter Karl Ulrich, in St Petersburg. September: Her mother leaves Russia.
1747	18	Catherine's father dies.
1752	23	Starts affair with Court Chamberlain Sergei Saltykov.
1754	25	September: Gives birth to son Paul.
1755	26	Affair with Polish aristocrat Count Stanislas August Poniatowski begins.
1757	28	December: Gives birth to daughter Anna Petrovna.
1758	29	Catherine's ally, Chancellor Aleksei Bestuzhev-Riumin disgraced and exiled; Poniatowski retuned to Poland.

Year	History	Culture
1729	Treaty of Seville between France, Spain and England.	J S Bach, 'St Matthew Passion'.
1739	Prince Potemkin born. Emperor Charles VI signs peace treaty with Turks.	David Hume, *A Treatise of Human Nature*.
1744	France declares war on England and Austria. Second Silesian War: Frederick the Great takes Prague.	'God Save the King' first published.
1745	French defeat British at battle of Fontenoy. Jacobite rebellion in Scotland.	Hogarth, 'Self-Portrait'.
1747	Prussian-Swedish alliance for mutual defence.	Voltaire, *Zadig*.
1752	Treaty of Aranjuez between Spain and the Holy Roman Empire.	Henry Fielding, *Amelia*.
1754	Anglo-French war in North America.	Hogarth, 'The Election'.
1755	End of Anglo-Austrian alliance.	Voltaire, *La Pucelle de Orleans*.
1757	Seven Years War: Frederick the Great defeats French at Rossbach and Austrians at Leuthen.	Gainsborough, 'The Artist's Daughter with a Cat'.
1758	Seven Years War: Russia occupies East Prussia; Battle of Zorndorf between Russians and Prussians.	Samuel Johnson begins weekly periodical *The Idler*.

Year	Age	Life
1759	29	March: Anna Petrovna dies.
1760	31	May: Catherine's mother dies in Paris.
1761	32	Catherine begins affair with Guards officer Grigory Orlov. Becomes pregnant. December: Empress Elizabeth dies; Catherine's husband the Grand Duke Peter declared Emperor Peter III.
1762	33	April: gives birth to Orlov's son Alexei. 28 June: Catherine, with aid of Orlov brothers and others, launches coup against Peter III and proclaimed Empress Catherine II in own right in Petersburg. Catherine herself rides at head of troops sent to arrest Peter. 29 June: Peter abdicates. July: Peter dies, supposedly from colic. 22 September: Crowned Empress in Moscow.
1763	34	Starts long correspondence with French philosopher and author Voltaire.
1764	35	Catherine confirms secularisation of Church lands. July: Abortive plot to free former Emperor Ivan VI from captivity ends in latter's death, killed by his guards. With backing of Catherine, Poniatowski elected King of Poland.
1765	36	Catherine already writing her 'Great Instruction' on the nature of government and laws in Russia.

Year	History	Culture
1759	Seven Years War: British capture Quebec from the French; Austrians defeat Prussians at Kunersdorf.	Voltaire, *Candide*.
1760	Seven Years War: Russians occupy Berlin. George III accedes to the British throne.	Sterne, *Tristram Shandy* Vols 1 and 2. Botanical gardens at Kew opened.
1761	Seven Years War: Austrians take Schweidnitz.	Collected works of Voltaire appear in English translation.
1762	Truce between Prussia, Saxony and the Holy Roman Empire.	Gluck, opera 'Orpheus and Eurydice'. Rousseau, *Du contract sociale...*
1763	Peace of Paris ends Seven Years War.	Voltaire, *Treatise on Tolerance*.
1764	Hyder Ali usurps throne of Mysore. Jesuits suppressed in France.	Voltaire, *Philosophical Dictionary*. Mozart writes first symphony at age eight.
1765	British pass Stamp Act taxing American colonies. Joseph II succeeds as Holy Roman Emperor.	Horace Walpole, *The Castle of Otranto*.

Year	Age	Life
1767	38	Cruise down river Volga to see part of her new empire. July: Presides over opening of new Legislative Commission in a bid to codify Russia's laws.
1768	39	Autumn: Ottoman Empire declares war on Russia over Catherine's involvement in war-torn Poland. Legislative Commission suspended.
1770	41	June: Celebrates Russia's naval victory over Turks at Chesme.
1771	42	Catherine alarmed by plague that kills tens of thousands of people in Moscow and provokes riots.
1772	43	Catherine's Russia plus Prussia and Austria agree Partition of Poland. Orlov replaced as official favourite by Alexander Vasilchikov.
1773	44	Under guidance of Catherine, Paul chooses German princess Wilhelmina as his bride; she converts to Orthodox Church and takes name Natalya. Welcomes French writer and philosopher Denis Diderot to Petersburg. Pugachev revolt.
1774	45	Lieutenant-General Grigory Potemkin installed as new favourite. Peace treaty ends war with Turkey, gives Russia access to Black Sea. Pugachev revolt ends.
1775	46	Catherine herself drafts statute that reorganises local administration throughout Russia.

Year	History	Culture
1767	American colonists in Boston make nonimportation agreement against British taxes. Jesuits expelled from Spain, Parma and the Two Sicilies.	Sterne completes *Tristram Shandy*.
1768	Citizens of Boston refuse to quarter British troops. Austria renounces all claim to Silesia.	Mozart, opera 'Bastien and Bastienne' first performed.
1770	'Boston Massacre': street brawl between citizens and British troops. Dauphin of France marries Marie Antoinette of Austria.	Gainsborough, 'The Blue Boy'.
1771	Gustavus III becomes King of Sweden.	First edition of the *Encyclopaedia Britannica*.
1772	Boston assembly threatens secession.	Choderlos de Laclos, *Les Liaisons Dangereuses*.
1773	Boston Tea Party: demonstration against tea duty. Jesuit order dissolved by the Pope.	The waltz becomes fashionable in Vienna.
1774	Louis XVI becomes King of France. American Continental Congress meets at Philadelphia.	Goethe, *The Sorrows of Werther*.
1775	Outbreak of American Revolution.	Sheridan, *The Rivals*.

Year	Age	Life
1776	47	April: Paul's wife Grand Duchess Natalya and baby die in childbirth.
		September: Paul chooses new German princess as bride, Sophia, who becomes Maria Fedorovna.
1777	48	December: Maria gives birth to son Alexander.
1779	50	April: Maria has second son Constantine.
1781	52	Catherine signs secret alliance with Emperor Joseph II of Austria.
1782	53	Catherine promotes new Police Code.
1783	54	Potemkin annexes nominally independent Crimean peninsula.
1784	55	Treaty of Constantinople: Ottoman Empire agrees to Russian annexation of the Crimea.
		April: Death of former lover Orlov.
		25 June: Sudden death of latest favourite Alexander Lanskoy.
1785	56	Catherine promotes two new reforms, the Charter to the Nobility and the Charter to the Towns.
1786	57	Statute on National Education.
1787	58	Catherine embarks on a tour of south of Russia to mark 25 years as Empress.
		August: Turkey declares war on Russia.

Year	History	Culture
1776	American Declaration of Independence.	Adam Smith, *An Inquiry into the Nature and Causes of the Wealth of Nations*.
1777	British army surrenders to Americans at Saratoga.	Sheridan, *The School for Scandal*.
1779	French ally with American rebels. Peace of Teschen ends War of Bavarian Succession. Spain declares war on Britain.	Samuel Johnson, *Lives of the Poets*.
1781	British capitulate at Yorktown.	Mozart, opera 'Idomeneo'.
1782	Peace talks between America and Great Britain.	Mozart, opera 'Die Entführung aus dem Serail'.
1783	Peace of Versailles: Great Britain recognises American independence.	William Blake: poetical sketches.
1784	British peace treaty with Tippoo Sahib of Mysore. India Act: East India Company under British government control.	Goya, 'Don Manuel de Zuniga'.
1785	Frederick the Great forms League of German Princes against Joseph II.	David, 'Oath of the Horatii'.
1786	Death of Frederick the Great.	Mozart, opera 'The Marriage of Figaro'.
1787	Establishment of US federal government. Parlement of Paris demands Louis XVI summon the Estates-General.	Schiller, *Don Carlos*. Mozart, opera 'Don Giovanni'.

Year	Age	Life
1788	59	Sweden declares war on Russia.
1789	60	Youthful guards officer Platon Zubov becomes new favourite. July: Catherine expresses alarm and dismay at French Revolution and plight of Louis XVI. Rewards Potemkin for 'multitude of victories' over Turks.
1790	61	August: Peace treaty with Sweden ends war.
1791	62	October: Potemkin dies. December: Peace treaty with Turks ends war, and extends Russia's access to Black Sea.
1793	64	January: Catherine breaks off relations with France after execution of Louis XVI. Second Partition of Poland. September: Senate proposes Empress be known as Catherine the Great. Grandson Alexander marries German princess Louisa Augusta, who is renamed Elizaveta.
1795	66	Third Partition of Poland.
1796	67	6 November: Dies in Winter Palace after massive stroke Son Paul proclaimed emperor. 5 December: On Paul's order, Catherine is buried side by side with exhumed remains of her late husband Peter III.

Year	History	Culture
1788	Austria declares war on the Ottoman Empire. US Constitution comes into force.	Goethe, 'Egmont'.
1789	Outbreak of French Revolution. First US Congress meets in New York. Austrians take Belgrade.	Blake, 'Songs of Innocence'.
1790	Death of Joseph II. Poland cedes Thorn and Danzig to Prussia.	Mozart, opera 'Cosi fan tutte'.
1791	Louis XVI arrested at Varennes.	Boswell, *Life of Johnson*. Death of Mozart.
1793	Execution of Louis XVI: the Terror begins in France. First Coalition against France formed.	Canova, 'Cupid and Psyche'. David, 'The Murder of Marat'.
1795	Directory takes power in France. Bonaparte made commander-in-chief of French forces in Italy.	Goya, 'The Duchess of Alba'.
1796	Bonaparte defeats Austrians in Italy. George Washington refuses to accept third term as US President.	Wordsworth, *The Borderers*.

Further Reading

Alexander, John T, *Catherine The Great* (Oxford University Press, Oxford: 1989): a scholarly and detailed assessment of Catherine's life that is especially interesting on the Empress' subsequent reputation and portrayal.

Cruise, Mark, and Hilde Hoogenboom, (translators), *The Memoirs of Catherine the Great* (Random House, New York: 2005): a chance to discover what Catherine wrote and thought in her own words.

De Madariaga, Isabel, *Russia in the age of Catherine the Great* (Weidenfeld and Nicolson, London: 1982): one of the most important scholarly works on Catherine and her impact on Russian history.

——, *Catherine the Great: a Short History* (Yale University, New Haven and London: 1990): a shorter, more readable version of the author's definitive work on the subject.

Dixon, Simon, *The Modernisation of Russia 1676-1825* (Cambridge: Cambridge University Press: 1999): one of the standard texts on the development of Russia up to the start of the 19th century.

——, *Catherine the Great* (Pearson, London; 2001): not a conventional biography but an assessment of Catherine's abilities as a leader and the issues she had to face.

Erickson, Carolly, *Great Catherine, The Life of Catherine the Great, Express of Russia* (Robson, London: 1994): a colourful and lively account of Catherine's life.

Goodwin, Jason, *Lords of the Horizons: A History of the Ottoman Empire* (Vintage, London: 1999): a very readable guide to the story of this empire.

Hartley, Janet M, *A Social History of the Russian Empire 1659-1825* (Longman, London: 1999): scholarly account of the social issues facing Russia before, during and after Catherine's rule.

Hosking, Geoffrey, *Russia: People and Empire, 1552-1917* (London: 1997): a lucid general history of Russia up to the revolution.

Hughes, Lindsey, *Peter the Great: A Biography* (Yale University Press, London and New Haven: 2002): an account of the life of one of the key figures in Russian history.

Lentin, A (ed), *Voltaire and Catherine the Great; selected correspondence* (Cambridge University Press, Cambridge: 1974): a guide to the important correspondence between Catherine and the French writer.

——, *Russia in the Eighteenth Century: from Peter the Great to Catherine the Great* (Heinemann, London: 1973): a concise and informative account of Russia in the 18th century.

Roberts, J M, *The Penguin History of Europe* (Penguin, London: 1996): a superb overview of European history that includes Russia's growing role in that story.

Rounding, Virginia, *Catherine the Great, Love, Sex and Power* (Hutchinson, London: 2006): very detailed and readable account of Catherine's life.

Sebag Montefiore, Simon, *Potemkin: Catherine the Great's Imperial Partner* (Vintage, London: 2005): an enthralling look at this most colourful and important of Russian statesmen.

Picture Sources

The author and publishers wish to express their thanks to the following sources of illustrative material and/or permission to reproduce it. They will make proper acknowledgements in future editions in the event that any omissions have occurred.

akg Images: p. 112; Berlin Film Archive: p. 138; Getty Images: pp. i, ii, 5, 7, 9, 12, 17, 24, 42, 51, 58, 63, 92, 105, 118, 130, 142; Topham Picturepoint: pp. 33, 39, 46, 65, 68, 85, 95, 100, 128.

Index

Note: family relationships are to Catherine the Great unless otherwise stated.